Additional Praise For *Always A Winner*

"Wouldn't it be great if we could accurately anticipate, understand, and proactively deal with economic challenges all the time? *Always a Winner* shows us how to do just that. Combining real-life corporate examples with easy-to-grasp economic theory, Peter Navarro provides you with all of the strategies, tactics and forecasting tools your organization needs to profitably manage through the ups and downs of the business cycle."

—*Ed Fuller, President & Managing Director*
International Lodging, Marriott International

"This compelling book offers strategies for coping with the business cycle from a keen observer and insightful commentator. Read it now in the midst of a recession, and read it again when the economy is several years into another expansion. That's when business needs to prepare for the next downturn."

—*Professor Edward Leamer*
Director, UCLA Anderson Forecast

"*Always a Winner* is required reading for every entrepreneur, money manager, and independent investor hoping to outperform the market and retire one day."

—*Mark T. Brookshire*
Founder of StockTrak.com and WallStreetSurvivor.com

"Our strategies of global diversification and broad product diversity coupled with an organizational culture keenly attuned to the importance of the business cycle to our bottom line has allowed Marubeni to survive for some 150 years. This book draws heavily on the experiences and lessons of companies such as ours to deliver a powerful set of strategies and forecasting tools to help your executive team move forward. *Always a Winner* will help your organization not just survive, but thrive, in today's turbulent economic environment."

—Teruo Asada
President and CEO, Marubeni Corporation

"Many businesspeople such as myself have learned the hard way that managing the business cycle for competitive advantage in today's fast-changing, globally-integrated economy is not only a must for survival but also the only sustainable strategy. In this very timely book, Professor Navarro clearly shows your executive team how to do just that – and always come out a winner!"

—Dr. Shankar Basu
Chairman & CEO, Toyota Material Handling, U.S.A., Inc.

Always A Winner!

Always A Winner!

FINDING YOUR COMPETITIVE ADVANTAGE IN AN UP-AND-DOWN ECONOMY

Peter Navarro

WILEY

John Wiley & Sons, Inc.

Library of Congress Cataloging-in-Publication Data
Navarro, Peter.
    Always a winner! : finding your competitive advantage in an up and down economy/Peter Navarro.
        p.   cm.
    Includes bibliographical references and index.
    ISBN 978-0-470-49720-3 (cloth : acid-free paper)
    1.   Business cycles.   2.   Industrial management.   3.   Gross domestic product.   4.   Recessions.   5.   Success in business.   I.   Title.
    HB3711.N38 2009
    658.4'012—dc22
                                                                    2009013303

Printed in the United States of America
10 9 8 7 6 5 4 3 2 1

To every business executive who got caught by surprise by the 2007 to 2009 crash—and who wants to make sure it never happens again

Contents

About the Author

Peter Navarro received his PhD in economics from Harvard University in 1986. Since 1988, he has been a professor at the Merage School of Business, University of California-Irvine.

Professor Navarro is a widely sought after and gifted public speaker. His unique and internationally recognized expertise lies in his big-picture application of a highly sophisticated but easily accessible macroeconomic analysis of the business environment and financial markets for investors and corporate managers.

Professor Navarro's books include the bestselling investment book *If It's Raining in Brazil, Buy Starbucks* and the pathbreaking management book, *The Well-Timed Strategy*. His most recent book is the bestselling *The Coming China Wars*, which takes a provocative look at the range of economic, political, and military conflicts likely to arise with the emergence of China as a superpower.

Professor Navarro is a regular CNBC contributor and has been featured on *60 Minutes*. He has appeared frequently on Bloomberg TV and radio, CNN, NPR, the BBC, and the *CBS Evening News*. His articles have been published in a wide range of publications, from the *Chicago Tribune, Los Angeles Times, New York Times, San Francisco Chronicle, Wall Street Journal* and *Washington Post* to *BusinessWeek*, the *Harvard Business Review*, the *MIT Sloan Management Review*, and the *Journal of Business*.

Professor Navarro is also an award-winning teacher and has recorded numerous audio lecture courses in the Modern Scholar series for Recorded Books. Sample titles include: *Big Picture Investing, Big Picture MBA*; and *Principles of Economics: Business, Banking, Finance, and Your Life*.

Each week, Professor Navarro publishes his "Well-Timed Strategy" newsletter on his Web site at www.peternavarro.com. This free newsletter provides timely economic and financial market analysis for both business executives and investors.

While Professor Navarro is an avid Dodgers baseball fan, his wife Leslie roots for the Angels. Opposites apparently do attract.

Other Books by Peter Navarro

The Coming China Wars: Where They Will Be Fought, How They Can Be Won (2008)

The Well-Timed Strategy: Managing the Business Cycle for Competitive Advantage (2006)

What the Best MBAs Know: How to Apply the Greatest Ideas Taught in the Best Business Schools (2005)

When the Market Moves, Will You Be Ready?: How to Profit From Major Market Events (2004)

If It's Raining in Brazil, Buy Starbucks: The Investor's Guide to Profiting From News and Other Market-Moving Events (2001)

The Policy Game: How Special Interests and Ideologues Are Stealing America (1984)

The Dimming of America: The Real Costs of Electric Utility Regulatory Failure (1984)

Preface

Most companies make a lot of money during economic expansions—and lose a lot of money during recessions. That is the way it has always been. That is the way it need not always be.

My job in this book is to show you how to be "always a winner" over the course of the entire business cycle—not just when economic times are good. To do this, I am going to arm you with all the strategies, tactics, and forecasting tools you will need to profitably manage your organization throughout the business cycle seasons—from the best of times to the worst of times.

The importance of learning to strategically manage the business cycle for competitive advantage was underscored some years ago by my chance encounter with Dwight Decker, a gentleman who at one point was one of the highest-flying tech executives in Orange County, California.

At the time of this encounter—at an Orange County meeting on homeland security—Decker was the CEO of Conexant, a semiconductor company spun off in 1999 from the defense company Rockwell. Within a year of that spin-off, Conexant's sales had rocketed up to more than $2 billion and its stock price had increased by more than sixfold.

Conexant's success was, however, ever so fleeting. Despite ample warning signs, Decker and his executive team failed to see the March 2001 recession and collapse of the tech bubble coming. When the company got caught with more than $1 billion of inventory write-downs and special charges, its stock price made a dizzying descent from almost $100 per share down to less than two bucks.

When I bumped into Decker at the homeland security meeting, I couldn't help but ask him how his company had failed to forecast the 2001 recession that had been its undoing. I then went on to provide a long list of leading economic indicators that had clearly signaled that recession.

Decker's reply absolutely floored me. He said: "We don't really pay any attention to that economic stuff. Our job is to make great new stuff and if we do that, the rest will take care of itself."

Unfortunately for both Conexant shareholders who lost billions of dollars and the thousands of Conexant employees who lost their jobs, no more naive words have ever been spoken. The message that Decker clearly failed to understand is that over the often-exhilarating ups and treacherous downs of the business cycle, economic ignorance will always eventually triumph over engineering brilliance.

A BIG-PICTURE VIEW OF THE ALWAYS A WINNER ORGANIZATION

Why Recessions Are More Dangerous than Any 10 Competitors

When a recession hits, the best surprise is no surprise.

—Ron Vara

A recession can do far more damage to your organization than any 10 competitors. That's a lesson I both regularly teach to my executive MBA students and preach to corporate audiences. Without question, it is one of the most important lessons that business executives around the world have all-too-painfully learned in the wake and carnage of the crash of 2007 to 2009.

Contrary to a popular view before that historic crash, the business cycle is not dead. Nor has this highly volatile and often destructive cycle even been tamed. This is a lesson sharply underscored by the culpability of America's own Federal Reserve and central banks around the world in helping to trigger the crash of 2007 to 2009 by first creating, and then perpetuating, a bubble global economy.

Because recessions can do far more damage to your organization than your competitors and because recessions will continue to be as inevitable as death and taxes, the 2007–2009 crash should serve as every business executive's epiphany about the need to recession-proof one's organization. The purpose of this book is to help you learn how to do just that.

The goal of this book is not, however, simply to teach you a valuable set of recession-proofing skills. More broadly, this book will also show you how to strategically manage your organization over the entire course of the business cycle—from the depths of a recessionary trough to the boom times of a robust economic expansion and back again. By learning to strategically manage the business cycle, your organization will be able to create a powerful competitive and sustainable advantage over your rivals and thereby find the grail sought by every executive team in the world: superior financial performance. In this way, you will be "always a winner."

CHAPTER 2

What Good to Great and Always a Winner Organizations Have in Common

Any organization can substantially improve its stature and performance, perhaps even become great, if it consciously applies the framework of ideas we've uncovered.

—Jim Collins, *Good to Great*

In 2001, just as the first recession in a decade was dawning on America, Jim Collins published a book called *Good to Great* that would go on to sell more than 4 million copies. The premise of Collins's book is exactly the same as the premise of this book: Companies that adopt a particular set of strategic business practices, that exhibit leadership reflective of those practices, and that build a supportive organizational structure and culture will enjoy superior financial performance.

In *Good to Great*, organizations such as Abbott Laboratories, Gillette, Nucor Steel, and Walgreens all shared in common "Level 5" leaders—self-effacing individuals with intense professional will who always put their company first. These organizations were also "Hedgehogs" that focused singularly and consistently on what they did best, pioneered the application of carefully selected technologies, embraced a culture of discipline, and, as a result of all of these elements, earned superior rates of return for their shareholders.

In this book, organizations such as DuPont, Johnson & Johnson, and Paccar all share in common "Master Cyclist" (short for "Master Business Cycle Manager") leaders who are global thinkers with a high degree of economic and financial market literacy and who are masters at strategically managing the business cycle. These organizations also have a strong "business cycle management orientation," and they deploy a wide range of forecasting capabilities to anticipate movements and key recessionary turning points in the business cycle. With a highly supportive structure and culture, these organizations then rely on their forecasting information to implement a set of often countercyclical business cycle management strategies and tactics in a timely way. In this way, these Master Cyclist organizations are not only able to recession-proof their shareholders and employees from the ravages of the business cycle, they also exhibit superior financial performance relative to their less-business-cycle-savvy rivals over the entire course of the business cycle.

ORIGINS AND METHODS OF THE MASTER CYCLIST PROJECT

It is no coincidence that *Always a Winner!* shares the same premise of superior financial performance with *Good to Great.* After reading Collins's book when it first came out, I and so many others were greatly impressed with Collins's insight and his compelling stories of great companies with sustainable superior performance. I was also impressed with both the research methods and the overarching question that Collins was seeking to answer: Why do some companies consistently outperform their rivals?

In fact, I had started the Master Cyclist Project at the University of California-Irvine just months before *Good to Great* was published to answer that very same question, albeit in the very different context of strategic management of the business cycle. After reading *Good to Great,* I was inspired to use a very similar research methodology. To that end, I assembled a large army of MBA students and immediately began an *extensive* set of case study analyses. Our initial Phase One goal was to identify the most effective strategies and tactics that could be applied over the course of the business cycle to improve financial performance.

In Phase Two, we conducted a supplementary set of more *intensive* case studies to identify those characteristics that separate Master Cyclist organizations that skillfully and proactively strategically manage the business cycle from Reactive Cyclist organizations that merely react, often far too late, to changing economic conditions. It was in this phase of the study that we identified the key characteristics of a successful Master Cyclist organization and its leaders. As noted earlier, these characteristics range from a strong business cycle orientation and an executive team with a high degree of economic and financial market literacy to a business-cycle-sensitive organizational structure and culture.

In Phase Three, we moved beyond individual case study analyses to a more rigorous statistical test of our hypothesized association between superior financial performance and skillful management of the business cycle. In this critical phase, we compared the stock price performance of 70 companies sorted into 35 "matched pair" rivals representing 35 subindustries in the Standard & Poor's (S&P) 500 Index over a five-year period going into and out of the March 2001 recession.

We chose the S&P 500 because it covers roughly three-quarters of U.S. corporations by market capitalization. Each matched pair of rivals in the sample consisted of a high- versus low-performing company in the industries and subindustries that make up the S&P 500—from aerospace, autos, and electronics to pharmaceuticals, railroads, and tires.

For example, one matched pair included the high-performing Walgreens versus the low-performing CVS. Another matched pair featured the high-performing Best Buy versus the low-performing Circuit City.

We chose the five-year period between February 1999 and December 2003 because it allowed us to compare how the rival companies in each matched pair first prepared for the onset of the 2001 recession by applying—or failing to apply—each of the Master Cyclist principles of strategic business cycle management identified in Phase One of the project. By extending the observation period two years after the recession ended, we were then able to measure the effects of the application of the various Master Cyclist principles on stock price performance.

In conducting this matched pair comparison, our working hypothesis was this: High-performing companies would implement strategic business cycle management principles more frequently than their low-performing rivals. In addition, low-performing companies would be more likely to exhibit Reactive Cyclist behaviors contrary to sound business cycle management principles; for example, while a high-performing Master Cyclist organization would countercyclically increase advertising during the recession, a low-performing Reactive Cyclist organization would cut advertising expenditures.

In fact, our study results provided strong support for this hypothesis. The overwhelming majority of high-performing companies were indeed much better at applying Master Cyclist principles than their low-performing Reactive Cyclist rivals. In this way, our study results established a very clear and strong statistical association between organizational performance and strategic business cycle management.

WHY ALWAYS A WINNER ORGANIZATIONS MUST BE MASTER CYCLISTS

Exhibit 2.1 illustrates how the Master Cyclist organizations in our sample dramatically outperformed their Reactive Cyclist rivals in terms of stock price performance and annualized returns. Specifically, this exhibit charts the growth—or lack thereof—of three separate $1 million investments from the start of our study period in February 1999, through the 2001 recession, and to the end of that period in December 2003.

The growth path of the first investment of $1 million illustrated in the exhibit is an investment in the market benchmark the S&P 500 represented by the popular exchange-traded fund with the ticker symbol SPY. The S&P growth path is represented by the middle line in the exhibit. Holding this broad market index through the period would have shaved about $70,000 off your initial investment and yielded a *negative* annualized return of 1.4%. Of course, that is what recessions do: They make it very hard to earn money in the stock market using a traditional buy-and-hold approach.

Exhibit 2.1   The Superior Performance of Master Cyclist Organizations

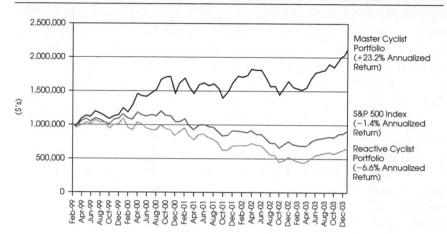

In contrast, if you had invested $1 million in a mutual fund comprised of the Reactive Cyclist companies, your investment would have lost more than 5% of its value on an annualized basis and been worth a mere $715,367 by the end period. This negative growth path—and loss of over $250,000—is represented by the lower line in the exhibit. It graphically underscores the point that recessions can be far more injurious to a company's bottom line than any 10 competitors.

Finally, if you had alternatively invested your $1 million in a mutual fund of the Master Cyclist companies at the start of the period, you would have earned a very robust annualized return of 23% right through the recession, and your portfolio would have been worth $2.1 million by the end of the December 2003. To borrow a phrase from Jim Collins, "You just gotta know how they did that."

WHAT JIM COLLINS MISSED

Now, here's the irony in basing the methods of the Master Cyclist Project on those of *Good to Great:* The superior stock price performance of the Master Cyclist companies clearly indicates that

Collins missed a very important factor when he failed to identify the robust performance effects of strategic business cycle management. In some sense, this is a forgivable sin. The study period that Collins used to gauge firm performance overlapped with one of the longest and most robust economic expansions in U.S. history—the roaring 1990s. During that time, the need for strategic business cycle management and any attendant recession-proofing of one's organization was extremely low.

The failure of Collins to consider the effects of business cycle turbulence on financial performance is underscored by the spectacular collapse of several of his Good to Great companies during the 2008 crash. The poster child for this problem has to be Fannie Mae, which saw its stock price plummet from more than $80 per share to less than a buck. In fact, Fannie Mae would no longer exist if it were not for a massive bailout from the federal government.

A second Good to Great company, Circuit City, provides a very interesting nexus between the sample of companies that Collins used in his book and the sample used in the Master Cyclist Project study. In particular, while Collins has Circuit City on the superior performance side of his ledger, our Master Cyclist research shows that the now-bankrupt Circuit City has played the business cycle management fool to a key rival and far more astute business cycle manager, Best Buy. Of course, the way to reconcile these two radically different assessments of Circuit City is simply to note that Collins found Circuit City to be a Good to Great company prior to the advent of the 2001 recession, and his study failed to anticipate that the vaunted Circuit City executive team would be an abysmal failure at recession-proofing the company.

Likewise, our research team found a third Good to Great company, Kimberly-Clark, on the other side of the performance ledger from Collins. The case analysis of this company has yielded one of the most interesting stories in the entire Master Cyclist Project. This is a story about how to price the business cycle exactly wrong.[1]

As explained in Chapter 19, the second worst thing a company can do in the middle of a recession is to raise its prices. However, the worst thing a company can do is try to hide those price hikes. Unfortunately, Kimberly-Clark's executive team tried to do just that.

In particular, during the 2001 recession, Kimberly-Clark tried to sneak a price hike on unsuspecting moms by reducing the product count in each package of its popular Huggies brand diapers. In a swift, tactical, Master Cyclist response, Kimberly-Clark's chief rival, Procter & Gamble, immediately cut prices on its competing Pampers brand and exposed Kimberly-Clark's deception in a massive ad campaign. The result was a considerable loss of both face *and* market share for Kimberly-Clark.

The point of these comparisons is not that Collins's work was bad or wrong. The organizational characteristics and leadership qualities that Collins identified in his research certainly do play a very important role in corporate performance. Rather, the point is that Collins missed a very important factor in not considering how companies strategically manage the business cycle as an element of performance. In doing so, he left his Good to Great companies vulnerable to the vagaries of recession and his conclusions open to failing the test of time.

The much broader point to be gleaned from the research of the Master Cyclist Project is this: To always be a winner, every organization should learn how to strategically manage the business cycle for at least two reasons. The first is a matter of defense and survival: The principles and practices of Master Cyclist management can teach any executive team how to recession-proof its organization in today's turbulent times—and thereby always be a winner.

The second reason to learn how to strategically manage the business cycle is a matter of sound offensive strategy. Recessions are often the very best times to attack one's rivals and seize both market share and the strategic high ground.

If, paraphrasing the words of Jim Collins leading off this chapter, your organization "consciously applies the framework of ideas" developed in the course of the Master Cyclist Project, it will "substantially improve its stature and performance" and "perhaps even become great."

Good to Great versus Always a Winner Organizations

Good to Great Attributes	Always a Winner Attributes
• "Level 5" self-effacing leaders with intense professional will that always put their companies first	• Global-thinking "Master Cyclist" leaders with a high degree of economic and financial market literacy
• "Hedgehogs" focused singularly and consistently on what they do best	• A strong "business cycle management orientation" and masters at strategically managing the business cycle
• Pioneer the application of carefully selected technologies	• Deploy a wide range of forecasting capabilities to anticipate movements and key recessionary turning points in the business cycle.
• Embrace a culture of discipline	• Organizational structure and culture strongly support and facilitate business cycle management activities
• Superior performance during economic expansions	• Superior performance over all phases of the business cycle

3

What Are the Three Steps to Becoming an Always a Winner Organization?

Recessions teach companies to be prepared even during the good times, because a recession is like a battle—when you're in it, it's almost too late to start training for it. If you're not prepared for it, you will pay for it.

—Leonard Jaskol, former Chairman and
CEO, Lydall, Inc.

Corporate profits are highly correlated with business cycle movements. According to more than 60 years of data for the U.S. economy, profits tend to rise fairly steadily during economic expansions and then fall very sharply during recessions. Moreover, this relationship holds true for almost 70% of all corporate activity.

The statistical fact that most companies suffer falling profits during recessions further reinforces the point that the business cycle can be far more destructive to a firm's bottom line than any 10 competitors. This observation alone should be enough motivation for every executive team in the world to pay far more attention both to forecasting the business cycle and to strategically managing its movements and key turning points.

The fact that at least some companies are able to maintain robust profitability during recessions likewise provides hope that there exists a set of strategies and tactics and a broader management method that allows these companies to "always be winners" over the entire course of the business cycle. This set of strategies and tactics and a broader three-step strategic business cycle management method is illustrated in Exhibit 3.1.

Exhibit 3.1   Master Cyclist Superior Performance Triangle

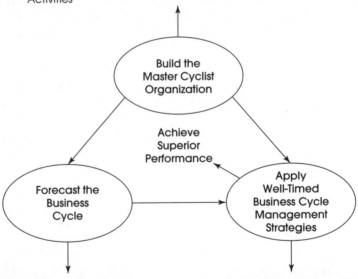

- Strong Business Cycle Management Orientation
- High level of Economic and Financial Market Literacy
- Organizational Structure Facilitates Forecasting and Strategy Implementation
- Organizational Culture Supports Business Cycle Management Activities

Build the Master Cyclist Organization

Achieve Superior Performance

Forecast the Business Cycle

Apply Well-Timed Business Cycle Management Strategies

- In-House Computer Models
- Outside Subscription Forecast Services
- Monitor the Shape of the Yield Curve
- Assess the Stock Market Trend
- Follow the Corporate Earnings Calendar
- Track the GDP Forecasting Equation!

- Production, Inventory, and Supply Chain Management
- Human Resources Management
- Advertising and Marketing
- Pricing the Cycle and Credit Management
- Capital Expansion and Modernization
- Acquisitions and Divestitures
- Capital Financing

This exhibit illustrates that in order to always be a winner, your organization must become a Master Business Cycle Manager by following these three steps:

Step One. Develop and deploy strong forecasting capabilities to anticipate movements and key turning points in the business cycle and effectively disseminate that forecasting information to key decision makers.

Step Two. Apply well-timed business cycle management strategies and tactics across the functional areas of your organization in a synergistic and integrative fashion in response to your forecasting data.

Step Three. Over the longer term, build your organization with a strong business cycle management orientation, an executive team with a high degree of economic and financial market literacy, and an organizational structure and culture that strongly support and facilitate all strategic business cycle management activities.

By following Steps 1 through 3, your organization will not only recession-proof itself when the business cycle comes crashing down, it will also gain a competitive advantage over its rivals while minimizing costs, maximizing profits, and increasing market share. In this way your organization will achieve superior financial performance and always be a winner over the entire course of the business cycle.

STEP ONE: DEVELOPING AND DEPLOYING A STRONG FORECASTING CAPABILITY

In order to anticipate movements and key turning points in the business cycle, your organization obviously must first develop and deploy a very strong forecasting capability. In this task, it is essential that your executive team move beyond any traditional reliance on either in-house computer forecasting models or outside subscription forecasting services. While such forecasting resources can be quite valuable in guiding your organization, the task of forecasting the business cycle cannot simply be delegated to some distant shop of economists. Instead, one of the cornerstone lessons of this book is this:

Every business executive must learn to become an astute business cycle forecaster!

To this end, in the process of training thousands of executive MBA students and corporate executives, I have developed a relatively simple but extremely powerful method of forecasting the business cycle that every would-be strategic business cycle manager can wholeheartedly embrace. As I shall explain in more detail in the next part of this book, all this forecasting method requires is a working knowledge of a relatively small number of forecasting tools, such as the bond market's yield curve and the gross domestic product (GDP) forecasting equation, and a disciplined commitment to applying these tools through a daily reading of the financial press. By using these tools, your executive team will *never* be caught by surprise by a recession again.

STEP TWO: APPLY WELL-TIMED BUSINESS CYCLE MANAGEMENT STRATEGIES

The Master Cyclist Project and its hundreds of case studies and statistical analyses of hundreds of corporations has revealed a comprehensive set of business cycle management strategies and tactics that can be applied over the course of the business cycle to gain competitive or sustainable advantage over your competitors. These Master Cyclist principles span the functional spectrum of the modern corporation—from production, inventory control, supply chain management, advertising and marketing, to human resources management, corporate finance, and acquisitions and divestitures. Each Master Cyclist strategy has been business cycle–tested by highly successful corporations both large and small around the world; and each has been shown to be very effective in enhancing financial performance.

In this regard, many of the Master Cyclist principles featured in this book are implemented countercyclically in the darkest days of a recession. Invariably, they encounter great resistance in Reactive Cyclist companies that lack a strong business cycle management orientation and the requisite skills to manage the business cycle.

For example, while most Reactive Cyclist companies *cut* advertising during a recession in a desperate effort to pinch pennies, the Master Cyclist organization countercyclically *increases* advertising to take advantage of lower advertising rates and less congestion in the advertising market. In this way, the Master Cyclist is able to cost-effectively build brand awareness while increasing market share and thereby garner a lot more revenue when the economy eventually turns.

The poster child and a classic example for building a brand through countercyclical advertising is Michael Dell and his brilliant countercyclical advertising coup d'état during the 1990–1991 recession. Seeking to build his fledgling company's brand and thereby break into the ranks of the big boys at the time, Michael Dell increased his company's advertising by more than 300% during the depths of that recession. Moreover, while Dell was radically ratcheting up his advertising budget, established players like Apple, IBM, and the now–dearly departed Digital were slashing their budgets by almost 20%. By seizing the recessionary day in this way, Dell was able to build both brand and market share and thereby set the stage for his company's brilliant ascent during the 1990s.[1]

In a similar fashion, while most Reactive Cyclist companies lay people off during recessions, the Master Cyclist human resources manager cherry picks from the much deeper recessionary labor pool to find highly talented staff at relatively lower costs. In this way, this well-timed human resources management strategy improves the quality of the overall organization.

An equally classic case in point is offered up by Avon's cherry-picking on a grand scale during the 2001 recession. As the economy headed south in 2001, Avon's executive team realized that this recession would result in "an ever larger pool of women"[2] to recruit to sell its cosmetics, perfumes, and other products. Avon's executive team also understood quite well that a recession was a great time to sell its products because during these tough times, many women would not be able to afford department store brands.

> To bring this talent into the company, Avon revitalized an old program called Sales Leadership in which the company's top performers are taught how to recruit, train, and supervise their own group of representatives. This program, coupled with a number of other equally aggressive initiatives, allowed Avon to expand its workforce by almost one third—or by roughly one million.[3]

This bold countercyclical hiring strategy had a very dramatic effect on Avon's performance over the next several years. On the strength of record profits, Avon's stock price rose by 16% in 2002 and another 25% in 2003 while sales rose dramatically.

It is important to note that strategic business cycle management principles typically are not just applied countercyclically. They also are implemented both synergistically and in a multidisciplinary fashion across the organization's many functional areas.

For example, countercyclical advertising in a recession not only helps the marketing department achieve its brand-building goals. It can also help the organization's supply chain managers trim any excess inventories that may build up during the recession.

STEP THREE: BUILDING THE MASTER CYCLIST ORGANIZATION

Structure follows strategy.

—Alfred Chandler

Forecasting the business cycle and applying well-timed business cycle management strategies and tactics in response to forecasting data represent the two bread-and-butter tasks of the strategic business cycle manager. Over the longer term, however, an equally important task is to build a solid Master Cyclist organization that will always be a winner—in good economic times or bad.

In this regard, the noted business historian and Harvard professor Alfred Chandler argued in his classic book *Strategy and Structure* that changes in strategy require companies to change their structure.[4] For an organization to become a truly effective strategic business cycle manager, it needs these four characteristics:

1. A strong business cycle management orientation
2. An executive team that is highly literate about macroeconomics and the financial markets
3. An organizational structure that facilitates the flow of forecasting data and timely decision making
4. An organizational culture that strongly supports all business cycle management activities

The term *business cycle management orientation* refers to recognition by the organization's executive team that recessions not only represent potentially extreme dangers. More broadly, movements and turning points in the business cycle also represent a potential source of competitive and sustainable advantage as well as an important determinant of both the flow and stability of future earnings.

Executive teams with a strong business cycle management orientation will be outwardly focused on economic movements and broader macroeconomic events. These teams will also seek a continuous in-flow of information from various forecasting resources, suppliers, and customers. In this way, a strong business cycle management orientation helps the organization forecast future demand for both resource planning and strategic purposes.

As an integral part of a strong business cycle management orientation, the Always a Winner organization must be led by an executive team with a high degree of *economic and financial market literacy*. Such literacy refers to the ability of an executive to understand everything from how fiscal and monetary policy work and why the stock market's trend and the bond market's yield curve are leading indicators of the business cycle, to how movements in interest rates, inflation rates, trade deficits, budget deficits, and exchange rates are all highly interrelated. And here's the crucial point about economic and financial market literacy:

> Only by achieving a high degree of economic and financial market literacy can an executive team correctly interpret forecasting data, accurately anticipate movements and key turning points in the business cycle, and apply strategic business cycle management principles in a timely way.

Beyond the need for a strong business cycle management orientation and a highly literate executive team, a true Master Cyclist organization must have a structure that facilitates the timely acquisition, processing, and dissemination of forecasting information. Such a structure must also facilitate the equally timely, synergistic, and integrative implementation of strategic business cycle management principles.

The chemical giant DuPont is the epitome of an Always a Winner organization structured to last through the up-and-down movements of the economy. In fact, DuPont is one of the very few major corporations that still maintain its own team of economists. It has also built an extensive set of forecasting models, has very formal channels of communication across its business units to process and disseminate the information, regularly communicates to shareholders on the role of the business cycle in determining earnings performance, and is led by a management team with the clear authority to respond quickly to the onset of a new business cycle event. Perhaps not coincidentally, DuPont tends to perform well over all phases of the business cycle—despite the highly cyclical nature of its businesses.

Beyond the need for a facilitative organizational structure, the Master Cyclist organization must also have an organizational culture that supports all of its strategic business cycle management activities.

The importance of a supportive *organizational culture* is illustrated by one of the best strategic business cycle managers in the world, Nucor Steel. As part of its cultural fabric, Nucor employees have embraced an innovative share-the-pain program. This program provides for voluntary salary cuts and reduced work hours when times are tough as a means of avoiding painful layoffs. In this way, Nucor is able to manage its production costs during downturns with little labor strife and without losing valuable talent.[5]

ACHIEVING SUPERIOR FINANCIAL PERFORMANCE

As you will learn in this book, some strategic business cycle management principles, such as countercyclical advertising, are designed to build brand and market share. Other principles, such as countercyclical inventory management and Master Cyclist corporate financing over the stock market and interest rate cycles, are designed to minimize costs. Still other strategic business cycle management principles, such as procyclical pricing, are designed to maximize revenues.

Together, these strategic business cycle management principles work in a synergistic and integrative way across the functional areas of your organization to maximize profits, minimize costs, and increase market share. In this way, strategic business cycle management allows you to protect your organization in bad economic times—and thereby always be a winner. In this way, strategic business cycle management also leads to superior financial performance. (For you younger managers reading this book, it may be useful to add here that by bringing this Always a Winner method to the attention of your CEO and top executives, you may also become the macroeconomic hero of your company—a title earned by many of my former MBA students.)

How to Strategically Manage Through the Business Cycle Seasons

We've had one of these [economic crashes] before, when the dot-com bubble burst. What I told our company was that we were just going to invest our way through the downturn, that we weren't going to lay off people, that we'd taken a tremendous amount of effort to get them into Apple in the first place—the last thing we were going to do is lay them off.

And we were going to keep funding. In fact we were going to up our R&D budget so that we would be ahead of our competitors when the downturn was over. And that's exactly what we did. And it worked. And that's exactly what we'll do this time.

—Steve Jobs, Apple CEO

This quotation from Steve Jobs on managing through the 2007 to 2009 crash perfectly captures the essence of strategic business cycle management in two key Master Cyclist dimensions—human resources management and the timing of capital expenditures. While most companies desperately lay off workers when a recession hits and promptly turn off the capital expenditures spigot, Master Cyclist executives like Steve Jobs understand the value of protecting workers during downturns and the strategic importance of counter-cyclically investing during a recession so as to be ahead of competitors when the downturn is over.

In this chapter, we are going to look beyond this specific wisdom of Steve Jobs and more broadly survey the entire strategic business cycle management landscape—from supply chain management, marketing, and pricing to human resources management, acquisitions and divestitures, and corporate finance. Our purpose is to acquire a broad overview of the strategies and tactics your organization can implement over the course of the business cycle to find competitive advantage in an up and down economy—and thereby be Always a Winner.

THE DYNAMIC PICTURE

Exhibit 4.1 illustrates how the various strategies and tactics of Always a Winner management can be applied over the course of the expansionary and recessionary roller-coaster movements of the business cycle. These strategies and tactics have been distilled from hundreds of case studies involving organizations of all shapes and sizes conducting business in locations all around the globe. They have all been battle tested over multiple turns of the business cycle.

The legend on the left side of Exhibit 4.1 identifies the major functional activities of the firm through which each of the Master Cyclist strategies and tactics are implemented. In the main body of Exhibit 4.1, the strategies and tactics associated with each of these firm functions are arrayed over the course of the business cycle to illustrate where their most timely application might be.

For example, at the trough of the business cycle, firms should countercyclically increase advertising. In contrast, toward the expansionary peak of the cycle, in anticipation of a recession, firms should tighten credit and aggressively collect accounts receivable.

With the dynamic picture of Exhibit 4.1 thus setting the stage, we now turn to a broad overview of each of the major principles of strategic business cycle management.

Exhibit 4.1 Always a Winner Strategies over the Business Cycle

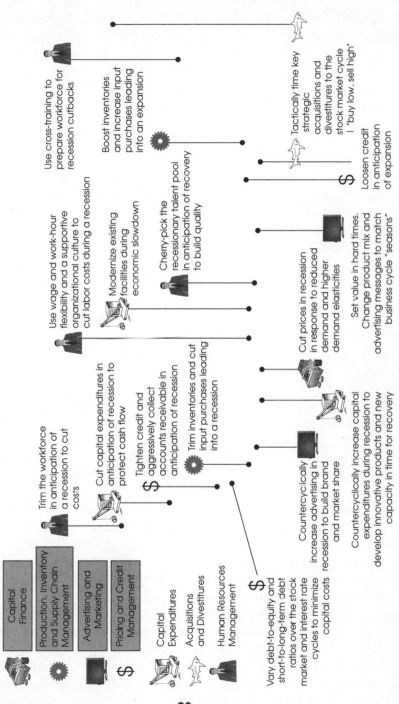

PRODUCTION, INVENTORY, AND SUPPLY CHAIN MANAGEMENT

> *AMD's losses included . . . a $227 million write-down of inventory, which lowered the company's gross margin 20 percentage points to 23%.*
>
> —*Information Week*

One of the most obvious symptoms of a failure to strategically manage the business cycle is the buildup of large inventories. Any company that gets caught with a large inventory overhang when a recession hits is likely to have to write down these inventories for a big loss. This is particularly true for high-technology companies, where products gathering dust in a warehouse quickly become obsolete. Just ask the semiconductor manufacturer Advanced Micro Devices, which had to write down more than $200 million in inventories during the 2007 to 2009 recession.

The worst part about trying to manage this inventory overhang problem is this: As the economy heads toward its red-hot expansionary peak, most organizations tend to increase production and build up even greater inventories in anticipation of an ever-upward-spiraling demand. This type of irrationally exuberant behavior is invariably driven by the naive belief that the good times will never end and by the natural desire never to be caught short of inventory.

A very costly variation on this theme is offered up by the luxury department store Saks Fifth Avenue. Even as recessionary storm clouds were already appearing, Saks chief executive officer (CEO) Steve Sadove sent his merchandisers jetting off to Milan and Paris to load up on inventory for the 2008 holiday season. The end result was a huge inventory pileup that forced Saks into steep price discounts and an equally huge loss on holiday sales.

In contrast to this typical Reactive Cyclist behavior, the astute strategic business cycle manager is even more vigilant about the dangers of a recession when economic times are at their very best. It is precisely at such boom times that oil prices, interest rates, wages, and inflation all begin rising sharply; and each of these factors or some combination of them are often harbingers of the next recession.

Accordingly, in anticipation of a recession, the strategic business cycle manager begins to trim both product inventories and the inventories of the raw materials and components necessary to produce the products. At this critical point, the risk of holding excess inventory heavily outweighs the risk of not having enough inventory to meet customer demand.

HUMAN RESOURCES MANAGEMENT

We prefer to keep our people together to withstand the crisis rather than making deep job cuts in a knee-jerk decision.
　　　　　　　　—David Sun, Chairman, Ernst & Young China

In a world in which workers have become just another commodity, many organizations ruthlessly slash their workforce when times get tough. This is exceedingly myopic behavior for a number of reasons. For one thing, it is very expensive to hire and train new workers. For another thing, the company that ruthlessly fires people at the first sign of trouble will face morale problems and suffer high turnover as soon as the job market improves.

There are much better ways to manage people over the course of the business cycle. If the desire is to trim labor costs during a recession, the time to start doing that is well before the recession hits. That means not only resisting the urge to continue hiring at premium wages well into the expansionary peak. It also means trimming the workforce in anticipation of a recession using such worker-friendly tools such as early retirement programs.

One company that failed to heed this sound advice leading up to the crash of 2007 to 2009 was the Internet services company Yahoo!. In the two years leading up to that crash, Yahoo! increased its workforce by almost 50% while paying premium wages. Of course, once the recession hit, Yahoo! had to lay off many of these very same workers. As the company tried to slash its bloated labor costs, it merely succeeded in crushing morale.

The Master Cyclist executive team not only avoids this recessionary trap—and any attendant mass layoffs and blows to morale. It uses the deepest and darkest days of a recession to cherry pick the very best new employees for its company from a talent pool now swollen with some of the very best and brightest from the industry.

That's exactly what Microsoft did in response to Yahoo!'s mass layoffs and plunging morale. In its most brilliant hire, Microsoft scooped up Qi Lu, a former top Yahoo search and marketing executive and pioneer in search engine technology and made him the president of Microsoft's Online Services. Through this kind of strategic cherry picking, Microsoft was able to acquire some of Yahoo!'s best assets—without actually having to pay a premium price for a company that it had once sought to acquire!

Beyond countercyclically hiring in the depths of a recession, there are other very important human resources strategies to mitigate and leverage business cycle risk as well. For example, during expansionary periods, it is very useful to conduct cross-training programs that build flexibility into your workforce. Cross-trained employees can shift seamlessly across different areas of the firm as demand ebbs and flows over the course of the business cycle. This is a strategy that companies such as AFLAC and Nucor regularly employ to preserve their workforce in downturns.

ADVERTISING AND MARKETING

When times are tougher, you've got to be more aggressive. Your growth has to come from market share captured from somebody else. You have to be a predator.
        —Britt Beemer, Chairman, America's Research Group

When recessionary times are tough, you indeed have to be a predator. Instead, the bean counters from accounting departments invariably make the rounds in Reactive Cyclist organizations and scream cut, cut, cut! Often, one of the very first things to *be* cut is the advertising and marketing budget. After all, aren't those things just frills?

In fact, there is a mound of research indicating that countercyclically increasing advertising during a recession is one of the fastest ways to build brand and seize market share. Not only are advertising rates cheaper, but there is far less congestion in the advertising market, and messages are thereby heard much more clearly.

Two companies that have astutely used this strategy to build brand and seize market share are Dell and Hyundai. During the 1990–1991 recession, a then-upstart Dell boosted its advertising by more than 300% while other companies like Apple and IBM were slashing their budgets by almost 20%. Dell built up its brand and dramatically increased its market share. This gambit perfectly positioned the company for its brilliant ascent during the 1990s.

During the 2007 to 2009 crash, Hyundai pulled off a similar marketing coup. While market leaders like GM and Toyota were cutting their advertising budgets, Hyundai's marketing department dramatically upped its budget to introduce the perfect advertising program for troubled times on the grandest of stages—the American Super Bowl.

Directly addressing the growing angst in America, Hyundai offered up its "Assurance Plus program" in which Hyundai promised to take back without penalty the vehicles of any buyers who lost their jobs. On the strength of this brilliant campaign, Hyundai enjoyed a big jump in sales while market leaders suffered a double-digit slump.

Of course, countercyclically increasing advertising during a recession doesn't mean you should simply pour more money into the very same marketing program you had in place before the downturn. Instead, as many companies have found, both the advertising messages and the product mix need to change to meet the changing moods of the business cycle seasons.

One company that clearly knows how to retool its product mix and sell value in a recession is Campbell Soup. During the 2007 to 2009 crash, Campbell's used an aggressive, countercyclical advertising campaign to remind its customers of the iconic product's value as a highly nutritious, low-cost meal. Comarketing its low-cost soups with Kraft cheese singles, Campbell's tagline was vintage Master Cyclist: "The wallet-friendly meal your family will love." Clearly, Campbell's countercyclical strategy paid off. It was the only company in the entire S&P 500 to show gains when the credit crisis first hit.

PRICING THE CYCLE AND CREDIT MANAGEMENT

Knowing the elasticity of demand for your products . . . is a key to determining pricing strategy.
—James Stotter, Founder, Busimetrics

In correctly pricing the business cycle, consider this scenario: A recession hits. Your revenues and profits plunge. Your shareholders are up in arms. Wall Street is punishing your stock. What do you do?

Unfortunately, the typical knee-jerk reaction is to raise prices to offset falling revenues. The equally inevitable result is that revenues fall even faster, and your company's balance sheets falls into a dangerous downward spiral. That's exactly what happened to Goodyear Tire during the 2001 recession when it desperately hiked prices not once but *three* times. The bottom-line results were disastrous.

This kind of desperate pricing behavior can happen only through a fundamental lack of economic literacy and a corresponding failure to understand one of the most important concepts in economics—price elasticity of demand.

The price elasticity of demand measures your product's sensitivity to price changes. For example, if a large price hike leads to an even larger percentage drop in consumer demand for a product, demand is said to be highly elastic in much the same way that a rubber band stretches significantly when you pull it. In such a case, any attempt to raise prices will lead to a fall in total revenues and a likely corresponding reduction in profits. This is because the revenue benefits of any price hike will be more than offset by the revenue losses due to fewer units sold.

A critical point here—and one that is rarely taught either in undergraduate economics or business school classes—is that price elasticities are *not* immutable. Instead, price elasticities generally become *more elastic* as a recession takes hold, thereby making products more price sensitive. That's why, as a Master Cyclist rule, you always want to be cutting your prices as the economy softens.

One company that has exhibited a very sophisticated understanding in the importance of the elasticity of demand in pricing strategy is Apple. At the initial release of its iPhone, Apple clearly understood that price would be highly *inelastic*, that is, very price insensitive. With customer interest at its peak, economic times good, and a huge pent-up demand for Apple's latest innovation, the company set the initial iPhone price at a whopping $599.

However, as the iPhone went into mass production and use and the economy softened, the executive team also understood that demand for the iPhone would become more and more elastic. To maximize its revenues, Apple therefore sequentially moved the iPhone price first to $399 and then to $199. Both unit sales and revenues continued to grow robustly—just as price elasticity theory predicts.

CAPITAL EXPANSION AND MODERNIZATION

Perhaps in no strategic business cycle management dimension is countercyclical behavior more important than in the planning of capital expenditures. Unfortunately, as regularly as the sun rises and sets, Reactive Cyclist organizations invariably cut capital expenditures during recessions—often dramatically—as the proverbial form of battening down the hatches. In fact, this is one of the worst strategic mistakes an organization can make.

In contrast, by countercyclically increasing your capital expenditures to build new plants and modernize existing ones, your organization will be first to market with products that reflect the latest innovations and styles. Moreover, this first-to-market effect is all the more amplified in higher-technology industries with shorter product cycles.

The reigning master of all Master Cyclists practicing this countercyclical investment strategy is Intel Corporation—the largest manufacturer of semiconductors in the world. As Intel's president and chief executive Paul Otellini has noted on the virtues of this strategy:

> New technology is what pulls companies in technology out of recessions. . . . We are making very long lead time investments. This new technology will lower our cost, and give us a more competitive product.[1]

Countercyclical capital expenditure programs have other advantages as well. One of the biggest of these advantages is that the costs of capital, construction labor, equipment, and raw materials all tend to be lower during a recession.

ACQUISITIONS AND DIVESTITURES

Hard times often come hand in hand with opportunities.
—Teruo Asada, President and CEO, Marubeni

"Buy low and sell high": That's the Master Cyclist mantra when it comes to executing your organization's acquisition and divestiture strategy.

While this seemingly simple recommendation would seem to make eminent good sense, far too many organizations refuse to follow it. That sad fact of Reactive Cyclist life is reflected in this observation: For any given acquisition or divestiture, there must always be both a buyer and a seller. By definition, one party to that transaction must always be getting its timing wrong and a bad deal—at least near stock market tops when stock prices are inflated and near market bottoms when stock prices may be undervalued.

One of the most darkly comic examples of a Reactive Cyclist buying high at the peak of a stock market bubble is offered up by the banking and financial services company Wachovia. It paid a whopping $25 billion for a subprime lender, Golden West Financial, at the height of the housing bubble. After that bubble burst, the weight of Wachovia's acquisition would ultimately drag it to the brink of bankruptcy and a shotgun marriage with Wells Fargo.

The darkly comic part of this example may be found in how Wachovia's CEO Ken Thompson described the acquisition. Prophetically—but in a way in which he never dreamed—Thompson grandly declared: "This is a *transformative* deal for us." Given that the deal forced Wachovia's assimilation into Wells Fargo, it was a *transformative* deal indeed.

In sharp counterpoint to Wachovia's massive miscue, there are Master Cyclists such as Micron, Oracle, and Warren Buffett's Berkshire Hathaway that have made a healthy habit of using recessions to pick up valuable assets on the cheap. Micron, for example, used the aftermath of the 2001 recession to buy a $2 billion chip factory from Toshiba for a mere $300 million. In even grander fashion, a cash-rich Oracle quietly went on a shopping spree during the depths of the 2007 to 2009 crash. It completed no less than 10 strategic acquisitions—all at bargain prices.

CAPITAL FINANCING

Shave a couple of hundred basis points off your capital costs over the course of the business cycle and save your organization millions of dollars. That's the mind-set every Master Cyclist brings to the capital financing table.

In this critical dimension, corporate finance teams have at least two parameters to optimize: the organization's debt-to-equity ratio and its ratio of short-term to long-term debt. Both of these parameters constantly change over the course of the business cycle and the related stock market and interest rate cycles. Only by strategically exploiting these cyclical changes in the debt-to-equity and short-term to long-term debt ratios in a timely way will your capital financing costs truly be minimized.

It should be clear from this overview that these Always a Winner strategies represent extremely powerful tools both to recession-proof your organization and to gain competitive advantage over your rivals. It should be equally clear that none of these strategies can be implemented over the course of the business cycle unless you and your organization have the ability to skillfully anticipate movements in, and key turning points of, that cycle.

It follows from these observations that in order to truly always be a winner, you must first learn to become your own economic forecaster. It is to this task—Step One in the Always a Winner management process—that we now turn.

STEP
I

BECOMING YOUR OWN
ECONOMIC FORECASTER

5

How (and Why) the Business Cycle Cycles

Bets on macroeconomic direction are among the biggest enterprises make. . . . Ignoring the macroeconomy and assuming that things will continue more or less as they are doesn't mean a big bet hasn't been made.

—Professor John S. McCallum

Before learning how to become your own economic forecaster, first it's useful to learn about both how and why the business cycle moves and the various forces that can trigger a recession. A useful starting point for this discussion is to introduce the most powerful forecasting tool featured in this book: the GDP forecasting equation.

GDP stands for "gross domestic product," and the economic growth of any nation is measured by its GDP. As a practical matter, GDP growth is driven by only four components: consumption, business investment, net exports, and government spending. As Chapter 6 explains, by using a select set of leading economic indicators and reports to track each of these major GDP components, any business executive can develop a very keen sense of the movements and key turning points of the business cycle. For now, however, the GDP equation can help us understand how to chart the business cycle and how the cycle moves through its different phases.

GDP CHANGES CHART THE BUSINESS CYCLE

When economists want to chart the path of the business cycle, they use percentage changes in the real, inflation-adjusted GDP to plot the cycle's major points over time. This technique is illustrated in Exhibit 5.1. Note that the stylized business cycle in the exhibit looks like a roller coaster. It illustrates that every business cycle sequentially moves through alternating expansionary and contractionary phases punctuated by key boom and bust turning points.

In plotting the business cycle, economists use the "real" (inflation-adjusted) GDP because it is the best measure of actual bricks-and-mortar growth. Adjusting for inflation solves the problem of having to compare one economy with a 5% GDP growth rate and zero inflation with another economy with a 10% GDP growth rate and a 10% rate of inflation. If inflation were not taken out of the GDP equation, it would look like the first economy was growing at half the rate of the second economy when, in reality, the second economy is not growing in real terms at all.

The real, inflation-adjusted percentage changes in the GDP not only help us chart business cycle movements. The quarterly and

Exhibit 5.1   Four Phases of the Business Cycle

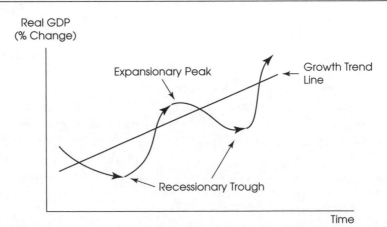

annual GDP growth rates also provide a very useful benchmark for the health of any economy.

For example, when the United States economy is growing at its full potential output and the unemployment rate is the lowest that rate can be without triggering inflation, the U.S. economy should be growing at about 3% to 4% annually. Anything short of that growth rate is considered slow growth or recession and is likely to lead to interest rate cuts by the Federal Reserve to try to stimulate the economy.

In contrast, a developing economy like that of China or India working from a much smaller economic base is capable of growing at a rate as high as 10% annually. In fact, China has experienced just such an astonishing annual growth rate for the better part of the last three decades. That's why at least for China, a fall in its GDP to only 5% effectively constitutes a recession.

WHY IS THE BUSINESS CYCLE SO HARD TO PREDICT?

There is at least one very important additional observation to make about the typical business cycle illustrated in Exhibit 5.1. The stylized picture of the roller-coaster business cycle in this exhibit may create the false impression that the business cycle always follows a fairly regular, and therefore easily predictable, pattern. In fact, just the opposite is true.

The problem forecasters face is that recessions are like sets of fingerprints—no two are alike. Some recessions exhibit a V-like pattern; They are very short but very deep. Such was the case with the 1957–1958 recession. Other recessions exhibit a more U-shaped pattern. These recessions may be either shallow or deep, but they are relatively longer and often more painful. Such was the case, for example, with the 1973 to 1975 recession, which lasted a full 16 months.

In addition, there is the dreaded W-shaped pattern; this signifies the so-called double-dip recession. Right after the economy recovers, it immediately falls prey to another recessionary drop. For example, while the 1980 recession was the shortest since World War II, the 1981 recession that immediately followed it to complete the double dip turned out to be the longest since the Great Depression.

Finally, there is the L-shaped recession. This type of recession is both deep and very long, which would be a fair description of the 2007 to 2009 crash.

It's not just that recessions are of varying lengths. So, too, are expansions. For example, the longest expansion in U.S. history was the so-called Clinton boom. It started just as Bill Clinton was moving into the White House in 1992; and it spanned almost the entire 1990s.

What is so very interesting about the Clinton boom from the perspective of protecting your organization during economic downturns is this: It was this very robust economic expansion in the 1990s that spawned a whole new generation of Reactive Cyclist business executives with little or no sensitivity to strategically managing the business cycle and little or no ability to recession-proof their organizations. After all, in such a robust economy, it was all too easy for these seemingly oblivious business executives not to think about recessions.

It was equally easy for these Reactive Cyclist business executives to come to believe, as many economists and business executives of that time actually did, that the business cycle had finally been fully tamed in the 1990s by the putatively wise policy makers running U.S. fiscal and monetary policy. As the 2007 to 2009 crash has taught us, however, hubris by any other name is still hubris—and the myth of a tamed business cycle has been forever shattered.

The broader point here is that the business cycle lacks what economists call "periodicity." Both the expansionary and recessionary phases can be either relatively long or short, and any recession can either be shallow or deep. It is precisely this lack of periodicity that makes the business cycle that much more difficult to forecast. (See "How Sun Spots (Don't) Forecast the Business Cycle" for an amusing look at one of the earliest and ill-fated efforts at prediction.)

WHAT ARE THE MAJOR RECESSIONARY TRIGGERS?

Now that we have a better understanding of *how* the business cycle moves, let's turn to the question of *why* the business cycle moves and, more precisely, how recessions can be triggered. To answer these questions, let's return to the GDP forecasting equation. It may be usefully represented as follows:

$$GDP = C + I + (X - M) + G$$

In this equation, C stands for consumption and I stands for business investment. The term $(X - M)$ represents net exports, which is simply the difference between the amount of exports, X (what a country sells to other countries), and the amount that country imports, M (what a country buys from abroad). Finally, G stands for government spending, and often, during a recession, the government is called on to be the spender of last resort to stimulate an economy out of the doldrums.

One reason why this GDP forecasting equation is such a powerful forecasting tool is that the right-hand side of the equation helps us keep a very close eye on four of the most important possible triggers of a recession. What I mean by that is this: Some recessions are consumer-led while others are business investment–led. Still other recessions can be triggered by a sharp decline in exports while some are the result of the inflationary effects of excess government spending and large budget deficits.

Consider the typical business-led recession. In this type of situation, business executives may be worried about rising interest rates, rising inventories, and the possibility of a recession. When these worries drive business executives to cut back on investment, they ironically induce the very recession they had feared. This is what happened, for example, to help trigger the business investment–led recession that began in March 2001.

In contrast, consumers worried about the effects of a war, a random terrorist act, a collapsing housing market, and/or rising gasoline prices may dramatically cut back their spending and thereby lead the economy into a recession. These were just some of the factors that help trigger the consumer-led crash of 2007 to 2009. Of course, once consumers begin to lead the economy into a recession by reducing their spending, business investment soon follows as inventories began to build, and businesses cut back on capital investment and begin layoffs.

A failure in the net export component of the GDP equation can be a third trigger for a recession. A classic case in point is offered up by the Great Depression. After the stock market crash in 1929, both the U.S. and the global economy began to slow sharply. As political discontent rose along with the unemployment rate, a wave of protectionist measures, such as the Smoot-Hawley tariffs, passed by the U.S. Congress washed over the world. The result was a steep decline in global trade.

This dramatic falloff in exports not only helped turn the GDP growth rates of many countries negative. It also helped turn what might have simply been a severe but relatively brief recession into the Great Depression.

When the fourth component of the GDP equation—government spending—triggers a recession, this is the most ironic situation of all. After all, according to the well-established doctrine of Keynesian economics, increased government spending is supposed to get us out of a recession, not put us into one. That said, a prolonged period of increased federal government spending—for example, to pay for a war in Vietnam or Iraq—may indirectly lead the economy into recession. This can happen if this prolonged fiscal stimulus creates a large budget deficit and a companion inflationary spiral and forces the Federal Reserve to hike interest rates dramatically to control inflation. It is precisely this fear that has so many economists worried about the U.S. government's trillion-dollar fiscal stimulus designed to "cure" the 2007 to 2009 crash.

ROLE OF OIL PRICE SHOCKS AND A BUMBLING FEDERAL RESERVE

While any one of the four components of the GDP forecasting equation can trigger a recession, all four of these components may be simultaneously subject to external shocks that can trigger a slowdown. In fact, one such type of shock—oil price shocks—have helped push the American economy into all six recessions since the 1970s.

For example, the recession of 1973 to 1975 was preceded by a tripling of the price of oil in the wake of the Yom Kippur war and Arab oil embargo. The double-dip recession of 1980 to 1982 was likewise preceded by a spike in price of oil precipitated by the Iranian revolution in 1979.

Oil prices similarly spiked prior to the 1990–1991 recession after Saddam Hussein and Iraq invaded Kuwait in 1990. Of course, both the 2001 recession and the 2007 to 2009 crash were also preceded by soaring oil prices.

As a sixth and final recessionary trigger—and file this one under high irony—there is the very same Federal Reserve that has been set up to prevent recessions. Here, as history has repeatedly taught us, an overaggressive and bumbling Federal Reserve may inadvertently trigger a recession through a series of ill-advised interest rate hikes. In this way, and as explained more fully in

Chapter 12, the Federal Reserve played a very key role in helping to trigger the March 2001 recession by helping to suppress business investment.

Here is the key takeaway from this chapter: Understanding that any given recession can alternatively be consumer-led, business investment–led, export-driven, triggered by misguided fiscal or monetary policies, or precipitated by a major exogenous shock such as a steep oil price hike, is a critical step toward developing your own forecasting capability. Having taken this critical step, we can now move to the next chapter and an overview of the forecasting toolkit that I am equipping you with. This economic toolkit will allow you to become a do-it-yourself (DIY) forecaster—one of the most important skills of the Always a Winner manager.

How Sun Spots (Don't) Forecast the Business Cycle

William Stanley Jevons was a respected British economist who (simultaneously with Carl Menger and Leon Walras) in 1871 developed the important Theory of Marginal Utility, a concept fundamental to modern economics and the other social sciences. He is less well known for his more wacky sunspot theory of the business cycle.

In 1878 Jevons published an article titled "Commercial Crises and Sun Spots" in the highly respected journal *Nature*. His research tracked over 100 years of crises by analyzing the accounts of the Bank of England, export data to India, corn prices, stock-jobbing scandals, and bankruptcies. He concluded that a British financial crisis occurred on average every 10.466 years and wrote that "fluctuations of the money market, though often apparently due to exceptional and accidental events, such as wars, great commercial failures, unfounded panics and so forth, yet do exhibit a remarkable tendency to recur at intervals approximating to ten or eleven years." Jevons tied this to the measurements of astronomer J. A. Broun, who clocked the solar sunspot cycle at 10.45 years.

Jevons speculated that sunspots represent a variation in solar energy output that impact plant growth and hence agricultural output. In his article and an earlier (1875) presentation to the British Association, he asserted that the price of commodity crops impacted consumer confidence and hence a variety of other businesses, result-ing in occasional "crises." Most interestingly, Jevons stated that the "crises usually happen in October and November"—a belief still firmly held by many modern traders and one supported by the fall disasters in 1929, 1987, and 2008.

Wacky though it was, the paper was one of the first academic discussions of the business cycle and most likely the very first to use an indicator to predict the cycle.

6

How to Forecast the Business Cycle in Four Easy Pieces

Give an executive team a forecast and guide it for a quarter. Teach an executive team how to forecast and guide it for a lifetime.

—Ron Vara

This variation on an old aphorism[1] aptly captures the value of learning how to become your own business cycle forecaster. Learning how to forecast is perhaps the most essential task of the Master Cyclist executive team. If your executive corps lacks the ability to anticipate movements and key turning points in the business cycle, all the business cycle management strategies in the world won't save your organization.

Traditionally, organizations have relied on one of two basic tools to meet their forecasting needs: either an in-house computer model or an outside subscription forecasting service (or both). One major downside of building and maintaining an in-house forecasting model is its high cost. That's why this option is more suited to larger organizations. It is also why during the halcyon days of the 1990s economic boom, many cost-conscious organizations eliminated their forecasting shops and fired their economists—a move that in hindsight has turned out to be penny wise and pound foolish.

As for outside subscription services, there is a plethora on the market. They range from private companies, such as Global Insight and Standard & Poor's, to academic institutions, including Georgia State and UCLA. While any one of these forecasting services may be valuable, one very efficient and low-cost option is to subscribe to the Blue Chip consensus forecast.

The Blue Chip consensus forecast represents an average of the forecasts of more than 50 of the top forecasting teams in the United States. Studies indicate that over the more than 30 years of its existence, the Blue Chip forecast has performed better than any single forecaster.

BECOMING YOUR OWN ECONOMIC FORECASTER

While any organization that is serious about forecasting the business cycle should use one (or both) of the traditional forecasting tools—an in-house model or an outside subscription service—this is merely the start, rather than the end, of your organization's forecasting duties. Indeed, one of the most important lessons I have learned over the last decade working with both executive MBA students and executive teams is that the task of forecasting the business cycle *cannot* be delegated to a remote group of economists. Rather, *every executive must learn to become his or her own business cycle forecaster.*

This may seem like a huge and complicated undertaking for executives who already have multiple responsibilities, but it really isn't as daunting as it sounds. In the process of training thousands of executive MBA students and corporate executives, I have developed a relatively simple but very powerful forecasting method. This method relies on the tools displayed in Exhibit 6.1. These tools include:

1. Monitoring the shape of the bond market's yield curve
2. Assessing the stock market's bullish or bearish trend
3. Following the corporate earnings calendar and, most important:
4. Tracking the GDP forecasting equation

Exhibit 6.1   Forecasting the Business Cycle in Four Easy Pieces

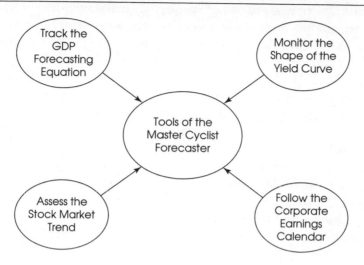

The bond market's yield curve defines the yield spread between short- and long-term government bonds. Normally, this yield curve slopes gently upward to reflect the higher risk of longer-term bonds. However, as I explain in more detail in Chapter 13, when the yield curve starts to slope downward, such a yield curve inversion provides a very strong recessionary signal. In fact, yield curve inversions have accurately predicted six of the last seven recessions with only one false signal.

The stock market is an only slightly less powerful financial market crystal ball. Stripped to its essence, all a stock price represents is an expectation by investors of a future stream of earnings. As I explain in more detail in Chapter 14, when stock market investors begin to anticipate a recession on the horizon, they also anticipate a fall in corporate earnings and begin to sell their stocks. That is why the onset of a bear market often also presages a recession; the onset of a bear market reflects the collective wisdom of investors that the economy will soon be heading south.

Following the corporate earnings calendar goes hand in glove with assessing the stock market trend. During the quarterly earnings seasons, all publicly traded corporations report their earnings as well as issue guidance for the coming quarters. While any one corporate earnings report reveals far more about a company than it does about the economy, collectively, the earnings reports of all companies—particularly major bellwether companies such as General Electric, General Motors, and DuPont—provide an excellent connect-the-dots portrait of the current state of the economy. Even more important, the *guidance* that firms offer during the earnings season about the trajectory of profits in the coming quarters often provides a very useful warning of potential recessionary clouds ahead.

While monitoring the shape of the yield curve, assessing the stock market's bullish and bearish trends, and following the earnings calendar are essential forecasting tasks, in order to truly become your own economic forecaster, it is important for you also to carefully track the GDP forecasting equation. Learning how to accomplish this all-important task is the subject of the next five chapters.

CHAPTER 7

Why the GDP Equation Is Your Most Important Forecasting Tool

The GDP [Report] is a must-read for many, because it is the best overall barometer of the economy's ups and downs. Forecasters analyze it carefully for hints on where the economy is heading. CEOs use it to help compose business plans, make hiring decisions, and forecast sales growth. Money managers study the GDP to refine their investment strategies. White House and Federal Reserve officials view the GDP as a report card on how well or poorly their own policies are working.
— Bernard Baumohl, *The Secrets of Economic Indicators*

This passage sharply underscores the importance of the GDP in the business cycle firmament. In fact, learning to track the GDP forecasting equation is without question the most essential task of the Master Cyclist executive.

My epiphany on the importance of tracking the GDP equation came almost a decade ago when I was preparing a keynote speech for a large corporate audience. My job in that speech was to provide an economic forecast for what would turn out to be a very stormy year.

I had delivered countless such forecasts in the past; and, increasingly, I had left these events with an uneasy feeling. My concern was that, like obedient sheep, far too many executives in the audience would use my forecast over the course of the next year for many of their decisions. If my forecast turned out to be wrong, these executives would likely make some very bad decisions.

My concern about the accuracy of my forecast—or lack thereof—did not reflect any fundamental lack of faith in my own abilities. Rather, my concern simply reflected the sober truth that any forecast is only as good as the underlying economic indicators and assumptions on which it is based. If, after a week, or a month, or a quarter, some aspect of the economic environment changed dramatically—consumer confidence dropped suddenly on war rumors, the Federal Reserve dramatically hiked interest rates on inflation concerns, or the European Union slapped steep protectionist tariffs on the United States—my sunny forecast might degenerate quickly into an economic quagmire.

In light of this concern, I realized that the only way I could truly help business executives was not just to give them a forecast to guide them for a quarter but to also teach them how to forecast to guide them for a lifetime. Since this epiphany, every time I now deliver an economic forecast, I also carefully explain how that forecast has been constructed.

The centerpiece of my forecasting method is the gross domestic product (GDP) equation introduced in Chapter 5. As Chapter 5 explained, a nation's economic output, or GDP, is totaled by adding the contributions of only four forces—consumption C, investment I, net exports $(X - M)$, and government spending G.

Now here is the punch line: By using a relatively select set of leading economic indicators and economic reports to track all five major components of the GDP equation, any business executive can anticipate movements and key expansionary and recessionary turning points in the business cycle. This forecasting method and the various economic indicators and reports used to track each GDP component are illustrated in Exhibit 7.1.

For example, to track the GDP itself on the left-hand side of the equation, you can use the Economic Cycle Research Institute (ECRI) Weekly Leading Index, which is released each Friday by the Economic Cycle Research Institute. In addition, for essential background reading, and for the reasons listed by Baumohl in the

Exhibit 7.1   Tracking the GDP Equation

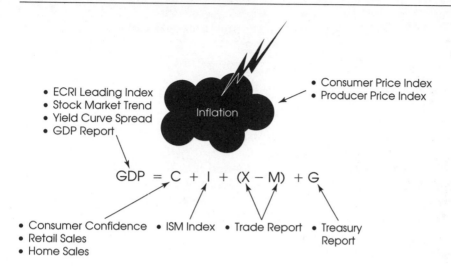

quotation leading off this chapter, you may also want to read the quarterly GDP report, which is issued by the U.S. Department of Commerce. Finally, as explained more fully in Chapters 13 and 14, both the stock market and bond market's yield curve spread are important leading indicators of the business cycle—and therefore movements in the GDP.

The ECRI index is an excellent broad measure of movements in the GDP for two reasons. It is specifically geared toward identifying key recessionary and expansionary turning points in the business cycle. It also has the best track record of any leading indicator in signaling recessions—regularly beating the competing and much better-known Index of Leading Indicators. In fact, the ECRI index has accurately signaled every recession since the 1990–1991 downturn with no false signals.

As for the composition of the ECRI Weekly Leading Index, two of its most important ingredients include two of the forecasting tools we discussed in Chapter 6: stock prices and the bond market's yield curve. In addition, the ECRI index also includes other critical indicators, such as changes in the money supply, mortgage applications, and initial jobless claims. Exhibit 7.2 illustrates the forecasting power of this index.

You can see that the ECRI index started a strong downward trend in June of 2007—a full six months before the recession

Exhibit 7.2   ECRI Leading Index Signals the Crash of 2007 to 2009

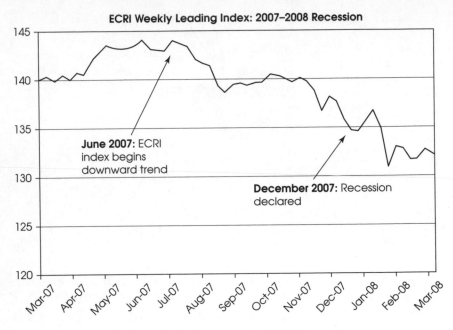

ECRI Weekly Leading Index: 2007–2008 Recession

June 2007: ECRI index begins downward trend

December 2007: Recession declared

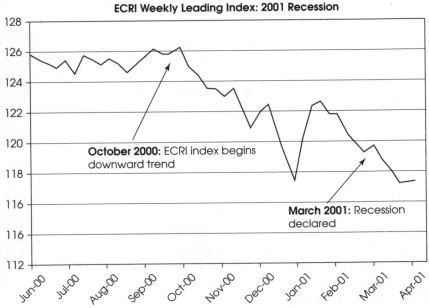

ECRI Weekly Leading Index: 2001 Recession

October 2000: ECRI index begins downward trend

March 2001: Recession declared

began. By December 2007, the ECRI index was at its worst reading since the 2001 recession.

The ECRI index likewise had similar success signaling the 2001 recession. It turned down in October 2000 and was in a very clear downward trend when the March 2001 recession hit.

WHY BOTHER TO TRACK THE OTHER GDP COMPONENTS?

Now, you may wonder at this point why it is useful to track each of the individual components of the GDP equation if the ECRI Weekly Leading Index is such a highly accurate leading indicator of the direction of the GDP itself in the broader business cycle. That's a great question, and the answer is simply this:

By individually tracking consumption, investment, net exports, and government spending, you will become a much more accurate forecaster and be able to spot recessions much sooner. The reason harks back to our discussion in Chapter 5 of the various possible triggers of a recession. Recall from that discussion that any given recession may be triggered by any one of the four forces driving the GDP. In this sense, tracking each of the individual GDP components serves as an early warning system.

In this regard, in many cases, a strong overall GDP growth rate may initially mask a marked deterioration in one of the GDP components. In such cases, a fall in consumer confidence or retail sales may alert you to the possibility of a consumer-led recession while a sharp downward move in the Institute of Supply Managers Index may be an early warning sign of an investment-led recession.

In a similar vein, by following the third component, you may spot a sudden fall in net exports due to weakening global demand or a strengthening currency that raises the specter of an export-driven downturn. Finally, by tracking the government spending component, you will be much more attuned to any possible growing dangers from a burgeoning budget deficit and a collateral possible inflation spike or interest rate hike.

Still another important reason to track the individual components of the GDP equation may be gleaned from this critical point: Even if the broad economy does not succumb to a recession, a fall in any one of the GDP components might hit your own organization very hard.

For example, companies in the air freight, trucking, and shipping industries are highly sensitive to changes in exports—and it's not just gross sales that are of concern. If you are a distributor of domestic products and the export trade slows, you will be able to go out and get better warehouse and logistical pricing.

For similar reasons, banking and finance companies must watch the GDP's investment component especially carefully; retail chains and consumer manufacturing companies must obviously be more keenly attuned to consumption patterns. Finally, companies in the defense and infrastructure-building industries will be relatively more affected by changes in government spending, so closely following the G in the GDP equation is de rigueur.

In the next four chapters, we take a more detailed look at the key leading indicators and reports used to track consumption, investment, net exports, and government spending, respectively. For now, let's end this chapter with a discussion of how to follow each of the leading economic indicators and government reports recommended in Exhibit 7.1.

HOW DO I FOLLOW THE ALWAYS A WINNER INDICATORS AND REPORTS?

The best way to follow the leading indicators and reports recommended in this book is by doing something that every business executive should do every business day anyway: Read the financial press. In fact, each of the recommended indicators and reports is covered extensively in publications such as *Barron's, the Financial Times, Investor's Business Daily,* and the *Wall Street Journal* as well as by financial news networks such as CNBC and Bloomberg.

Note, however, that when I teach this forecasting method to executive MBA students and business executives, I also strongly recommend that they supplement their reading and viewing of the financial press with some very targeted Web surfing. Specifically, I recommend the supplementary use of a Web site known as the Dismal Scientist.

The Dismal Scientist Web site is a product from Moody's Economy.com. Without question, it is the platinum standard for analysis of the monthly macroeconomic calendar of leading indicators and economic reports. The Dismal Scientist provides a one-stop shop for any executive serious about becoming a business cycle forecaster.

The very good news here is that through a very special arrangement with Moody's Economy.com, every reader of this book is entitled to a free one-month subscription of the Dismal Scientist. To sign up for this offer, just go to www.economy.com/dismal/navarro. At this special link, you will also be able to monitor the set of indicators and reports recommended in this book.

Action Item

Before moving on to the next chapter, you may want to log on to the Dismal Scientist Web site at www.economy.com/dismal/navarro and sign up for your free trial subscription. Once you have done this, read the latest reports for the ECRI Weekly Leading Index and the GDP report. As you review this information, ask yourself whether the ECRI Weekly Leading Index is signaling recession or expansion.

8

Why Tracking the Consumer Is the Ultimate Confidence Game

The Conference Board index of consumer confidence unexpectedly declined in December and is now at an historic low. . . . With consumer confidence shattered, the risks to the outlook for spending. . . are heavily weighted to the downside.

—www.economy.com/dismal

Whether humans descended from the apes or not, one thing is certain: The consumer is the 800-pound gorilla in the gross domestic product (GDP) forecasting equation. In developed economies like those of the United States and Europe, consumption accounts for fully two-thirds of all economic activity. Without a healthy consumer, it is virtually impossible for any economy to enjoy sustained growth.

In terms of what consumers actually spend, the consumption pie breaks down in this way: More than 50% of all consumer spending is on services—from dental care and doctors, to haircuts and home insurance. Another 30% of consumer spending is targeted at so-called nondurable goods—everything from food and shoes, to gasoline and (for anybody with a death wish) cigarettes. The remaining roughly 15% of consumer spending is on durable goods, such as furniture, refrigerators, and, pun fully intended, one of the biggest drivers of the U.S. economy, cars and trucks.

In order to properly track the consumption component of the GDP equation, it is useful to think in three dimensions.

1. How much is the consumer willing to spend? This is a function of the consumer's mood and confidence.
2. How much can the consumer afford to spend? This depends on the consumer's "budget constraint," which is a function of *both* the consumer's income *and* wealth.
3. What is the consumer actually spending his or her money on? Is it big-ticket items, such as cars and houses, or, fearful of a recession, are consumers shifting their spending patterns toward nondurable goods, such as food and medicine?

ARE YOU IN THE MOOD TO SHOP UNTIL YOU DROP?

The consumer's mood is of paramount important because fearful consumers are far less apt to open their wallets than confident and happy ones. The panoply of fears that perennially haunt consumers range from war, terrorism, and oil price shocks to a collapsing housing market, a paralyzing credit crisis and, what is often the mother of all worries, winding up on the unemployment line.

In theory, you have two options[1] to track the consumer's mood. The Consumer Confidence Index is published monthly by the Conference Board while the Consumer Sentiment Index is published twice a month by the University of Michigan. In practice, either measure will do because the two are highly correlated—they move together about 90% of the time.

Exhibit 8.1 illustrates how the beginning of a downward trend in consumer confidence helps signal both the 2001 recession and the crash of 2007 to 2009.

At the top of Exhibit 8.1, you can see that consumer confidence began to trend down as early as October 2000. This was a full five months before the onset of the March 2001 recession.

In the bottom part of the exhibit, you can see a similar pattern. Consumer confidence hit a peak in July 2007 and then trended

Exhibit 8.1 Forecasting Power of Consumer Confidence

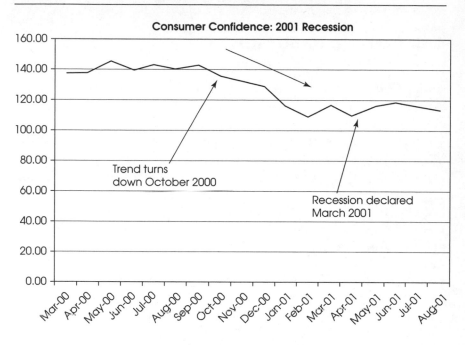

Consumer Confidence: 2001 Recession

Trend turns
down October 2000

Recession declared
March 2001

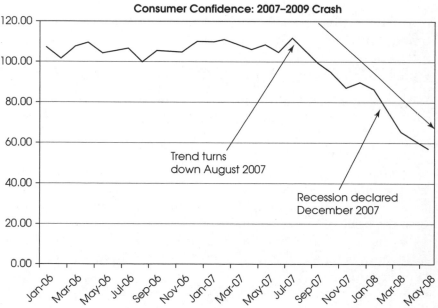

Consumer Confidence: 2007–2009 Crash

Trend turns
down August 2007

Recession declared
December 2007

steadily downward well in advance of the December onset of the crash of 2007 to 2009.

CAN I AFFORD TO BUY THIS?

Beyond the mood of the consumer, it is useful to look at the consumer's budget constraints. On the income side, if you want more detail, you can follow indicators such as personal income and consumer credit. Given that our goal in developing a forecasting method is to keep it as simple as possible, I prefer to follow the monthly progress of what consumers actually spend. The best indicator here, and one of the most important of all of the leading indicators, is *retail sales*, which are reported monthly.

The Department of Commerce collects the retail sales data using a monthly survey of almost 15,000 retail establishments of all sizes and types across the country. About 35% of the sales are of durable goods, such as autos, building materials, furniture, and home appliances. The remaining receipts come from the sale of nondurable goods: clothing and apparel, drugs, gasoline, food, liquor, mail order, and other general merchandise.

The retail sales report is important because it provides the first major evidence of consumption patterns for the month. For this reason, it is generally regarded as the most timely indicator of broad consumer spending patterns.

PARAMOUNT IMPORTANCE OF WEALTH EFFECTS

While income is an important driver of consumption patterns, over the last decade, so-called "wealth effects" have been even more influential. This is particularly true in an era in which wages have largely been stagnant. The idea of a wealth effect is that if the value of a consumer's stock portfolio or home rises, that consumer—now feeling wealthier—is likely to spend a lot more money than a consumer who has just taken a big hit in the stock market or who has seen the price of his or her home plunge.

A case in point is offered up by the stock market boom in the 1990s and its bust in the year 2000. At the height of the stock market's irrationally exuberant bubble, consumers spent far more robustly than their wages would justify. This was because of the increased wealth reflected in their rising stock portfolios. Of course, when the stock market bubble burst, the bull market's positive wealth effect turned sharply negative, consumers pulled in their spending horns, and, in this way, a negative wealth effect contributed to the 2001 recession.

Interestingly enough, history soon repeated itself. In the era of historically low interest rates following the 2001 recession, consumers benefited from another positive wealth effect in the form of rapidly rising home prices. In this housing bubble economy, many consumers used very aggressive mortgage refinancing effectively to turn their homes into ATMs while many other consumers flipped houses and speculative investment properties for large capital gains. Using this housing bubble wealth, consumers were able to spend at rates far in excess of what their wages would justify. Of course, when the housing bubble collapsed, the resultant negative wealth effect played a key role in triggering the crash of 2007 to 2009.

BIG- OR LITTLE-TICKET ITEMS?

This discussion provides a natural segue for our consideration of the final leading economic indicator to track consumer spending.[2] The important thing to consider here is whether the consumer is opening his or her wallet for big-ticket, interest rate–sensitive durable goods, such as vehicles and homes. At the trough of a recession, interest rates typically have fallen significantly, and there is considerable pent-up demand for these big-ticket items. At the first hint that a recession might be over, consumers therefore are likely to jump feet-first into the vehicle and housing markets to take advantage of these low prices and low interest rates. In this way, these two sectors are often pulling the U.S. economy out of its recessionary doldrums.

Exhibit 8.2 illustrates how a downward trend in new home sales helped signal the onset of the consumer-led crash of 2007 to 2009 crash but not the onset of the investment-led 2001 recession.

You can see clearly in the exhibit that new home sales were fairly steady leading into the investment-led recession of 2001 and thus provided no early warning sign of that recession. The lesson from this "recessionary dog that didn't bark" is to reiterate that it is critical to watch leading indicators for all components of the GDP forecasting equation, not just one component such as consumption.

New home sales leading into the crash of 2007 to 2009 do tell a very different story, however. In Exhibit 8.2, you can see that new

Exhibit 8.2   Forecasting Power of New Home Sales

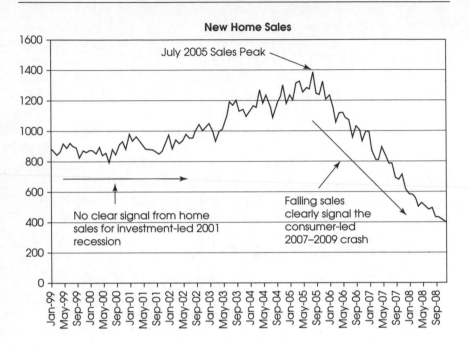

home sales hit a peak as early as July 2005 and then began to trend steadily downward. In light of the importance of the positive wealth effect associated with the housing bubble in propelling consumer spending at this time, this downward trend in new home sales would have been a very ominous sign of a possible impending consumer-led recession to a Master Cyclist executive.

Action Item

Log on to the Dismal Scientist Web site at www.economy.com/dismal/navarro and read the latest reports for consumer confidence, retail sales, and new home sales. Assess whether these reports signal expansion or recession. If you have additional time, compare the consumer confidence report with the consumer sentiment report.

Why Taking the Pulse
of Business Investment Is
as Simple as ISM

*This is a business-led recession. . . . There has been six or
seven months of noninvestment.*
              —Don Wainwright, CEO, Wainwright Industries

Business investment accounts for only about 15% of the gross
domestic product (GDP). However, what it lacks in size, it more
than makes up for in sudden volatile drops that are every bit
as capable of triggering a recession as the 800-pound gorilla of
consumption.

Conceptually, business investment can be divided into two categories: fixed investment and inventories. *Fixed investment* includes
everything from new factories and office buildings, to computer
equipment, machine tools, and assembly-line robots. *Inventories* are
what pile up when a recession hits and what get depleted during a
robust economic boom. In general, it is the fixed investment component of the GDP that strongly drives economic growth; inventory
levels help signal the relative strength or weakness of the economy.

In a typical business investment–led recession, executives will cut back sharply on capital expenditures for any number of reasons. Most obviously, they may see a broad buildup of inventories that suggests a slowing economy. More subtly, they may see the Federal Reserve aggressively raising interest rates to fight inflation and believe it is only a matter of time before the Fed's overaggressive actions trigger a recession. Beyond these worries—worries that the famous depression-era economist John Maynard Keynes once dubbed the "animal spirits" of the corporate community—business executives may be spooked by the outbreak of a war, which they fear will dampen consumer spending.

Regardless of why the business community's animal spirits may turn sour, once business investment starts to slow down, this negative trend is likely to accelerate. Ironically, in this way, the fears of the business community and its collective behavioral response in cutting business investment often become a self-fulfilling prophecy—a cautionary cutback in investment by worried executives triggers the very recession that executives fear.

A "ONE-STOP-SHOP" BUSINESS INVESTMENT INDICATOR

While it is important to understand all of the possible reasons why business executives may cut back sharply on business investment and thereby lead the economy into a recession, in the end, what really matters from a forecasting perspective is whether business investment is expanding or contracting. To answer that question, there is only one key leading economic indicator that you really need to follow: the so-called ISM Manufacturing Index published monthly by the Institute for Supply Management.

The Institute for Supply Management is the largest supply chain management association in the world, and the monthly release of its ISM index data is eagerly awaited by business and government leaders as well as the financial markets. This is because the ISM index has had an excellent track record signaling business investment–led recessions.

The ISM Manufacturing Index itself is based on a survey of purchasing managers in more than 300 companies representing over 20 industries in all 50 states. It is designed to measure the relative strength or weakness of the manufacturing, or supply side, of the economy at any given time.

In the purchasing manager survey, ISM respondents indicate whether there has been an increase, a decrease, or no change in the key components of the ISM Manufacturing Index. These key components include new orders, production, inventories, inflation, and slow delivery performance.

Now, from a business cycle forecasting perspective, here are the two most important things to note about the ISM Manufacturing Index.

1. The index is a "diffusion index" measured on a scale of 0 to 100. Any ISM index reading above 50 indicates that both the manufacturing sector and the economy are expanding. In contrast, any reading below 43 indicates that both the manufacturing sector and the economy are likely to be in a recession. Finally, any reading between 43 and 50 represents a significant recessionary signal.
2. The *farther* the ISM index is away from 50, the *faster* is the rate of change and the stronger the recessionary signal. This means that if the index goes below 35, as it did during the depths of the crash of 2007 to 2009, the economy is contracting at a much faster rate than if, say, the index is at 44.

A TALE OF TWO RECESSIONS

Exhibit 9.1 illustrates the strong predictive power of the ISM index—but only when it comes to investment-led recessions like the recession that started in March 2001.

On the left-hand portion of the exhibit, the ISM index begins trending down in December 1999 and falls below 50 in September 2000. This move below 50 was a full seven months before the onset of the investment-led 2001 recession. Moreover, by January 2001—two months before this investment-led recession began—the index had fallen precipitously, to 42. In this way, the ISM index provided a very powerful signal of the coming March 2001 recession.

Now contrast this powerful recessionary signal with the behavior of the ISM Manufacturing Index leading into the consumer-led

Exhibit 9.1   ISM Manufacturing Index and a Tale of Two Recessions

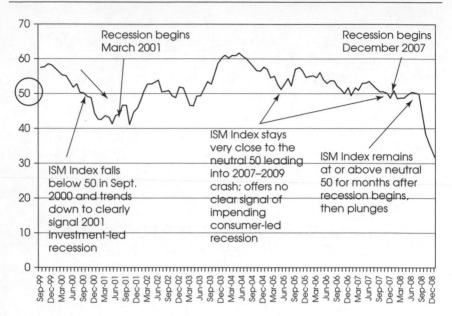

crash of 2007 to 2009 shown on the right-hand part of the exhibit. In the 24 months preceding the official start of that crash in December 2007, the ISM Manufacturing Index remained above 50 for all but two months. In those two months in which the ISM index fell below 50, it still registered a reading above 49 and very close to the neutral line. Thus, if you had been watching only the ISM index during this period, you would have been lulled into a sense of false security about the economy.

In this regard, it is perhaps even more interesting to note that *even after the recession of 2007 to 2009 officially began* in December 2007, the ISM index hovered only slightly below 50 for many months—very near the neutral mark. Finally, however, once the full force of the consumer-led recession gripped the manufacturing sector, the ISM Manufacturing Index fell off a cliff, plunging to 43.5 in September 2008. By the end of the year, it had fallen to 32.4—its lowest reading since 1980.

The broader point of this tale of two recessions is that it is critical to follow individual components of the GDP equation in order to spot early triggers to possible recessions in these individual components. The ISM index is a great indicator—but *only* for investment-led recessions.

Because of its success in signaling past investment-led recessions, the ISM index should be one of the most important weapons in your personal forecasting arsenal. Other government reports, on everything from durable goods and factory orders, to business inventories and capacity utilization, are important auxiliary reports; the ISM index is really the only economic indicator that busy executives need to use to track the business investment component of the GDP equation.

Action Item

Visit the Web site of the Institute of Supply Management at www.ism.ws and read more about the ISM index. Then log on to the Dismal Scientist Web site at www.economy.com/dismal/navarro and read the latest report on the ISM Manufacturing Index. Is the index pointing toward an expansion or a recession?

10

How Falling Exports Can Flatten an Economy in a Flat World

It's a tale of two economies—one propelled by robust growth in exports tied to strongly emerging markets overseas, the other mired in recession as consumers at home struggle to cope with record high debts, soaring energy prices and falling home prices.

The divergence could be seen clearly Thursday in a Commerce Department [trade] report showing a 1.9 percent spurt in export-led growth in the spring quarter even as many Americans say the economy is in the worst condition in decades and is shaping their attitudes during the campaign season.

The report showed that the domestic economy shrank at a 0.5 percent rate in the last quarter even as a 9.2 percent surge in exports and 6.6 percent drop in imports enabled the overall economy to eke out a gain.

—Washington Times

In an age of globalization and an increasingly flat world, the ultimate fate of any nation's economy often is ultimately determined by that nation's level of exports and imports and whether it is running large and chronic trade deficits. The reason is that, like a crooked college hoopster, chronic trade deficits shave critical points off the gross domestic product (GDP) growth rate.

To understand how a trade deficit can ultimately tip a nation's economy into recession, it's important to remember the definition of the term *net exports*. Net exports represent the difference between how much a country exports and how much it imports.

On the plus side of the GDP ledger, a nation's exports make a positive contribution to economic growth by creating jobs. On the negative side, however, when the United States, for example, meets its growth needs by buying foreign imports from another country, such as China, U.S. consumers may benefit from lower prices and more choices. However, it is China that enjoys the benefits of increased jobs, wages, and GDP growth. That's why, at least in this sense, international trade can often be a zero-sum GDP game.

Given the power of net exports to serve as both a short-term recessionary tipping point and a longer-term drain on economic growth, it is essential for business executives to track this critical GDP component regularly. Unfortunately, this task is not quite as easy as tracking consumption and business investment. This is because net exports cannot be monitored accurately by a few leading economic indicators, such as consumer confidence or the Institute for Supply Management index. Instead, each month, you must carefully scrutinize the monthly trade data and, most important, put any changes in imports or exports into their appropriate context.

WHY CONTEXT IS KING

Context is king in interpreting the trade data because in any given month, both exports and imports can rise or fall for any one of a number of reasons. For example, U.S. exports might rise because of rising growth in Europe and Asia—that's an expansionary signal. However, U.S. exports might rise because of a plunge in the value of the dollar, and that is much more of a mixed signal. Only by understanding the current context for any change in the net export data can you interpret this change as an expansionary or recessionary signal.

The best way to reinforce this critical context-is-king point is to walk through a number of different scenarios to show you how to interpret the latest trade news. Before we do that, however, let's first acquaint ourselves with the essential source of our data, the monthly International Trade report for the United States.

The Department of Commerce releases the International Trade report around the twentieth of every month. This critical report contains detailed information on imports, exports, and the trade deficit as well as trade flows by categories and countries. Upon the release of this report, the news media typically focus primarily on the top-line trade balance data, specifically whether the U.S. trade deficit has been rising or falling. From a forecasting perspective, that is only half of the story. The other half is to carefully scrutinize the growth patterns of both individual exports and imports.

Looking past the top-line trade deficit results at the export data is important because it allows you to assess whether U.S. companies are gaining or losing competitive advantage in the international arena. Looking at rising or falling exports also helps shed light on whether the economies of America's trading partners are strengthening and increasing their export demand for U.S. products or vice versa.

It is equally crucial to scrutinize the import data carefully. Rising or falling imports shed considerable light on the underlying strength of the domestic economy. For example, rising imports can be a sign that the U.S. economy is expanding at a more rapid rate.

Exhibit 10.1 illustrates the rapid growth in America's chronic trade deficit since 1992. In the figure, the first thing that should jump at you is the growing gap since 1992 between the top black line measuring imports and the bottom gray line measuring exports.

In fact, this trade deficit gap between U.S. imports and U.S. exports now amounts to more than $60 billion per month. Every year, this very large and chronic trade deficit shaves anywhere from one-half to one percentage point of growth off the U.S. GDP growth rate. And note here that while reduction of one-half to one percentage point in the GDP may seem like a small loss, that shrinkage is on an annual GDP growth rate for the United States that barely hits 4% even at full employment. Indeed, such a loss translates into a loss of more than $3 trillion over the last 20 years.[1]

Now, here is what is perhaps even more interesting about Exhibit 10.1. While the recession began in December 2007, robust export growth continued between December 2007 and July 2008. As the quotation from a *Washington Times* news dispatch leading off

Exhibit 10.1   America's Growing Trade Deficit Gap

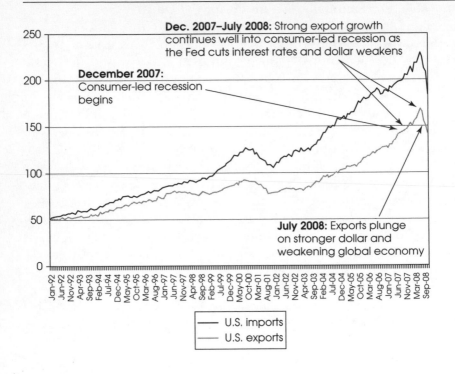

this chapter explained, this robust export growth helped to sustain the U.S. economy long after beleaguered consumers had led the country into a recession.

Note also in the exhibit that this robust export growth was in large part fueled by Federal Reserve interest rate cuts. As the Fed desperately cut rates to jump-start the faltering economy, the dollar steadily weakened and gave U.S. exporters an edge in the international trading arena.

However, once the worst financial crisis since the Great Depression erupted in full bloom in July 2008, the United States became a "safe haven" for foreign capital; and the dollar once again strengthened. This stronger dollar, together with a significant weakening of the global economy, led to the very sharp plunge in exports visible in the exhibit. The result was a significant deepening of the recession.

As with our analysis of the ISM Manufacturing Index in Chapter 10, these observations underscore the importance of watching all four components of the GDP equation to anticipate business cycle movements accurately.

AROUND THE WORLD IN FIVE SCENARIOS

Let's return now to the overarching theme of this chapter—context is king—when interpreting the monthly trade data as we turn now to a discussion of five International Trade report scenarios. The first two scenarios share in common rising exports. However, only the first scenario signals a continued economic expansion; the second scenario provides an early-warning sign of a possible global recession.

In a similar vein, the third and fourth scenarios share in common rising imports. Because rising imports shave points off of the GDP equation, both scenarios may seem bearish. However, in at least one scenario, quite the opposite conclusion may be drawn.

Finally, the fifth scenario helps explain how chronic trade deficits helped set the stage for the crash of 2007 to 2009.

Scenario One: Rising Exports Signal Continued Expansion

In Scenario One, the economies of both Europe and Asia are growing robustly, and European and Asian demand for U.S. exports is rising. In this scenario, rising exports provide a very strong signal of a likely continued economic expansion.

Scenario Two: Rising Exports Signal a Beggaring of Thy European Neighbor

In Scenario Two, both the U.S. and European economies are weakening. As a policy response, the U.S. Federal Reserve cuts interest rates. However, because the European Central Bank is more concerned about inflation, it does not match the Fed's interest rate cut.

As U.S. interest rates fall, the dollar falls relative to the euro. This is because foreign investors leave U.S. shores seeking higher returns in Europe. As the dollar/euro exchange rate turns more favorable for the United States, the United States sells more of its exports and imports fewer European goods.

The falling dollar thus helps to bolster the U.S. economy in the short run. However, over the longer term, as European exports fall because of a stronger euro, the U.S. Fed's policy serves only to further weaken the European economy. Eventually, as the European economy falls into recession, U.S. exports to Europe decline as well, a favorable exchange rate notwithstanding, and the United States likewise succumbs to recession.

Scenario Three: Rising Imports Signal There's a Party Going On

In this scenario, imports are rising because all the other three GDP components—consumption, business investment, and government spending—are hitting on all cylinders, and the U.S. economy is expanding robustly. As the economy booms, Americans have more income and wealth to spend, and they spend a proportion of that on more imports from Europe, Asia, and elsewhere. In this scenario, rising imports do not shave any significant points off the GDP growth rate but merely reflect a very robust expansion at the economy's full potential output.

Scenario Four: Rising Imports Make that Giant Sucking Sound

This much darker scenario involves a long-term rise in imports and a concomitant increase in America's chronic trade deficits. In fact, this scenario closely mirrors the economic history of the George W. Bush administration that helped set the stage for the crash of 2007 to 2009.

During Bush's presidential tenure, beginning in 2001 and ending in 2009, many U.S. manufacturers either shut down or moved their production facilities offshore, principally to China. Indeed, during this time, the United States lost millions of manufacturing jobs to China.

U.S. manufacturers were attracted to China not only by cheap labor but also by a complex web of illegal export subsidies that made it highly advantageous to manufacture in China rather than in Michigan or Ohio or California. Over time, this loss of America's manufacturing base would *directly* shave considerable points off the GDP growth rate through rising imports. However, the offshoring of American jobs also *indirectly* lowered the GDP growth rate by suppressing domestic business investment as U.S. companies diverted their investment dollars to China.

Eventually, over time, as job losses mounted in the manufacturing sector and American incomes grew stagnant, reduced spending by financially strapped consumers further eroded the GDP growth rate. This weakening of all three nongovernment sector components of the GDP equation—consumption, investment, and net exports—helped set the stage for the crash of 2007 to 2009.

Scenario Five: An Oil Price Shock Drains the Lifeblood Out of the Economy

This scenario likewise helps explain the role of the trade deficit and the onset of the crash of 2007 to 2009 even as it demonstrates one of the most important points about properly analyzing the International Trade report. This important point is that it is essential to carefully segregate the impacts of petroleum imports from the rest of the import-export equation.

Conceptually segregating oil imports from total imports is necessary because oil imports constitute almost half of the total dollar value of U.S. imports. Because of its dominance in the import column, even small changes in oil prices can obscure important movements in the non-oil segment of the U.S. trade deficit.

In this scenario, the Federal Reserve has once again cut interest rates to stimulate a weakened U.S. economy. As in Scenario Two, the result has been a collateral devaluation of the dollar and a welcomed stimulative increase in U.S. exports. However, because international oil prices are denominated in dollars, every time the dollar falls in value in response to lower U.S. interest rates, oil prices rise. In this way, the Federal Reserve's easy money policies and concomitant fall in the dollar lead to a precipitous increase in oil prices.

Now, here's the rub: Because the demand for imported oil is highly inelastic (meaning that consumers don't cut back much on their consumption when prices rise), America's oil import bill soars due to rising oil prices even as U.S. exports rise in response to the falling dollar. In this case, any expansionary benefits from rising U.S. exports gained from the cheap dollar are totally offset by the rise in America's import bill. While the total trade deficit remains unchanged, consumers have been hammered by the oil price shock. Eventually, this oil price shock—triggered by the Federal Reserve's misguided attempts to stimulate the economy—drags the United States into a recession.

SUMMING IT ALL UP

It should be clear from these five scenarios that properly analyzing America's International Trade report and, more broadly, understanding the roles of differing trade patterns as potential recessionary triggers require a much higher degree of economic and financial market literacy than interpreting other elements of the GDP forecasting equation. Indeed, to understand the messages of the International Trade report, it is critical to understand such complex relationships as those that exist among interest rates, inflation, oil prices, exchange rates, and trade flows as well as basic economic concepts such as the price elasticity of demand (explained in Chapter 19). This is precisely why, in an era of globalization, every business executive must commit not just to becoming his or her own economic forecaster but also to improving his or her own economic and financial market literacy.

Strong versus Weak Dollar

Strong U.S. Dollar	Weak U.S. Dollar
Fed rate hikes drive dollar up.	Fed rate cuts drive dollar down.
Inflation falls (imports less expensive).	Inflation rises (imports more expensive).
Dollar rises, oil prices fall.	Dollar falls, oil prices rise.
Trade deficit *rises* (exports fall, imports rise).	Trade deficit *falls* (exports rise, imports fall).
Consumers win, exporters lose.	Consumers lose, exporters win.

Action Item

Log on to the Dismal Scientist Web site at www.economy.com/dismal/navarro and read an analysis of the latest International Trade report. Look carefully at both the trade deficit numbers and the growth—or lack thereof—in imports and exports. Does this latest report signal expansion or recession?

11

Why Uncle Sam Is the Spender of Last Resort

We start 2009 in the midst of a crisis unlike any we have seen in our lifetime. . . . .Nearly two million jobs have now been lost. . . . Manufacturing has hit a twenty-eight-year low. Many businesses cannot borrow or make payroll. Many families cannot pay their bills or their mortgage. Many workers are watching their life savings disappear. And many, many Americans are both anxious and uncertain of what the future will hold. . . . If nothing is done, this recession could linger for years.

—President Barack Obama

This type of rhetoric from President Barack Obama was used to justify passage of the largest fiscal stimulus package in U.S. history immediately after he took office in 2009. Obama's rhetoric has deep roots in the teachings of famous British economist Lord John Maynard Keynes. His heavy reliance on stimulative government spending also has much in common with Franklin Delano Roosevelt's New Deal policies of the 1930s, which Keynes advocated as the way to get America out of the Great Depression.

During the Great Depression, Keynes argued that the broad macro economy, unlike individual markets, was not a self-correcting mechanism. In a severe recession or depression, fearful consumers will save more and spend less, wary business executives will conserve cash rather than invest, and a soft global economy will make any export-driven recovery impossible. Thus, when a fall in consumption, business investment, or net exports triggers a recession, increased government spending must ride to the rescue. In this way, government spending must be the spender of last resort in the gross domestic product (GDP) growth equation.

It was on this foundation of Keynesian economics that FDR launched the New Deal and its massive public works projects to jump-start the economy. It is on this same foundation of Keynesian economics that governments around the world today have justified the implementation of massive fiscal stimulus programs to recover from the crash of 2007 to 2009.

From the perspective of trying to manage an organization or company, this kind of Keynesian fix creates all sorts of strategic problems in both capital financing and production planning. At the core of these problems is the need for governments to run ever larger budget deficits to finance their fiscal stimuli. As a practical matter, there are only two politically feasible ways to finance such burgeoning deficits: sell bonds or print money (with higher taxes generally not possible politically).

DANGERS OF DEFICIT FINANCING

The problem with selling government bonds to finance the budget deficit is that the selling of government bonds can "crowd out" corporate bonds in the bond market and thereby reduce business investment in the GDP growth equation. How does such crowding out happen?

In order for the U.S. Treasury Department to sell its deficit-financing bonds to the private market, it has to raise interest rates sufficiently high to attract investors. However, these higher government interest rates draw investors away from the corporate bond market and thereby draw precious financial capital away from organizations such as yours!

The ultimate irony of such bond financing is that as the government tries to stimulate the GDP through increased spending, any stimulative effects may be offset by a fall in business investment. It is in this way that increased government spending crowds out private investment; and this crowding-out effect is all the more pernicious because government spending is usually far less efficient in propelling an economy than private sector investment.

The alternative to selling bonds and suffering this crowding-out effect is to print money to finance the budget deficit. This printing of money doesn't happen quite literally. Rather, it happens when the Federal Reserve purchases the deficit financing U.S. Treasury bonds *before* they go to the open market.

When the Fed buys the Treasury Department's deficit-financing bonds before they get to the private bond market, it is said to be "accommodating" the government's fiscal policy. This is because the Fed is buying the bonds rather than letting them compete with corporate bonds on the open market.

This method of financing the budget deficit is equivalent to printing money because the Fed simply pays for the Treasury bonds with a check that increases bank reserves. Banks, in turn, then lend out more money out based on these increased reserves, so the effect is to increase the money supply.

One short-run benefit of the print money option is to *lower* interest rates—the direct opposite result of bond financing, so business investment actually may be stimulated. However, over time, this expansionary monetary policy is highly inflationary.

Eventually, to fight the inflation caused by the excess printing of money, the Fed has to start raising interest rates. At this point, the clear danger will once again be a recession triggered by a fall in business investment and a fall in the purchases of interest-rate-sensitive consumer durables, such as cars and housing. That's why when the Fed starts printing money to finance fiscal policy, your organization should be very worried about the future path of the economy.

SIZE AND TIMING PROBLEMS

The dangers of increasing government spending to fight a recession do not end with how the resultant budget deficits are financed. There are also well-known size and timing problems. On the size issue, it's very difficult to calculate exactly how much fiscal stimulus is needed: too little doesn't get the job done, too much ignites inflation.

On the timing issue, it takes a lot longer for government spending to work its stimulative magic than for monetary policy to stimulate the economy. This is because all the new infrastructure the government wants to spend its money on to jump-start the economy may not be shovel-ready, that is, ready for immediate construction. Instead, most of the planned infrastructure will take significant time to plan and build.

Now, here is a clear danger from this timing problem—and the reason why monetary policy typically is preferred to stimulative fiscal policy: Because the full impact of the fiscal stimulus may not come soon enough to help a faltering economy, initially the fiscal stimulus may be ineffective. Over time, however, as other factors, such as falling interest rates and falling oil prices, help the economy recover, eventually once again full employment is reached. At this point, however, the effects of the fiscal stimulus may continue to build—and here is where irony is in full bloom.

Indeed, at this ironic point, the fiscal stimulus—initially designed to help the recessionary economy recover—winds up overheating the fully recovered economy and causes inflation. This inflation, in turn, forces the Federal Reserve once again to begin raising interest rates. If the Fed raises interest rates too far too fast, another recession will ensue—this one caused by the original fiscal stimulus and its unintended inflationary consequences.

Because of these myriad problems, it is critical for you and your executive team not only to monitor government spending closely but also to understand the broader implications of the government's reliance on massive fiscal fixes for the future trajectory of inflation and interest rates and the possibly reduced ability of the economy to grow robustly over the longer term. This observation again underscores the need for every executive team to build up its economic literacy in order to best manage the organization.

HOW TO TRACK GOVERNMENT SPENDING

The best way to monitor government spending is to review the U.S. Treasury Budget report on a monthly basis. This report provides a running estimate of the annual budget deficit as economic conditions change.

Exhibit 11.1 provides a snapshot of a typical year in the revenues and expenditures life of the United States featured in the Treasury Budget report.

Exhibit 11.1 A Year in America's Budget Deficit Life

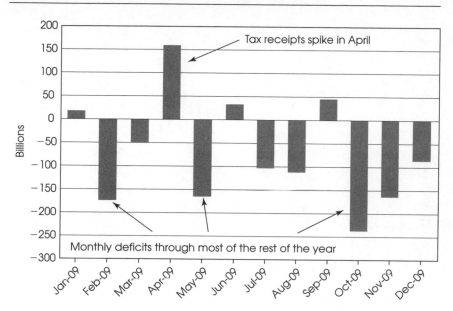

You can see in the exhibit that in most months, the budget is in deficit; that is, government spending well exceeds tax receipts. You can also see that the only month in which the government runs a huge surplus is, not surprisingly, that very same month in which we all file our annual tax returns: April, the cruelest month for our bank accounts.

Exhibit 11.2 graphically illustrates that chronic budget deficits have been an unnerving fact of U.S. economic life for almost 50 years. Indeed, since 1960, the United States has run only six budget surpluses, with four of them coming at the end of the Clinton administration, from 1998 to 2001.

More specifically, the exhibit indicates that the budget deficit first ballooned in the 1980s, under the Republican administrations of Ronald Reagan and then George H. W. Bush. After inheriting a significant budget surplus from Bill Clinton, President George W. Bush proceeded to break all budget deficits through his embrace of tax cuts and heavy war expenditures plus, as he left office, the burden of recession.

Exhibit 11.2   Budget Deficit History of the United States

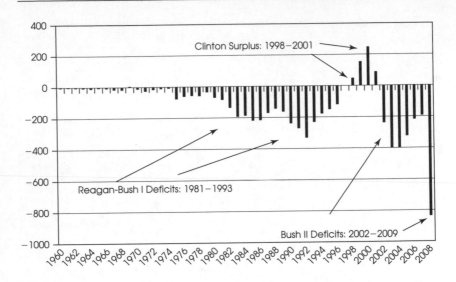

Today, as the U.S. government and governments around the world continue to up the fiscal stimulus ante dramatically—and the U.S. debt burden rockets past $12 trillion—the world is faced with a ticking budget-deficit time bomb of unprecedented proportions. The bottom-line implication of this gloomy longer-term picture is that, over time, *chronic budget deficits are likely increasingly to threaten your organization's ability to borrow capital at reasonable interest rates.*

Budget deficits also can be highly inflationary; and once such deficit-induced inflation hits, the Federal Reserve must respond with interest rate hikes that will hamper your ability to raise capital and likely will trigger a recession. For all these reasons, it is critical that you and your executive team closely monitor the U.S. Treasury Budget, report on a monthly basis.

STRUCTURAL VERSUS CYCLICAL: A DISTINCTION WITH A DIFFERENCE

To end this chapter, I want to leave you with one last economic literacy builder that should help you in your analysis of the government spending component of the GDP forecasting equation. This literacy builder involves understanding the crucial difference between a structural and a cyclical deficit.

A *structural deficit* is that part of the actual budget deficit that would exist even if the economy were at full employment. When the United States runs a structural budget deficit, it is spending beyond its means. Any attempt to increase government spending in the presence of a large structural budget deficit can end only in a nasty inflationary spiral.

In contrast, a *cyclical deficit* is that part of the actual budget deficit attributable to a recessionary economy. A cyclical deficit results from a combination of reduced tax revenues and the increased income transfer spending that kicks in during a recession on such things as unemployment compensation, food stamps, and other welfare benefits.

The good news about a cyclical deficit is that it can be eliminated by actually increasing government spending and temporarily running a bigger budget deficit. This fiscal stimulus magic works because once the economy gets back to its full employment output, tax revenues increase, welfare payments are reduced, and this technical deficit comes back into balance.

The bad news about a structural deficit is that it can be eliminated only by either raising taxes or cutting spending. If a government tries to increase government spending in the presence of a structural deficit, the inevitable result must be either higher interest rates (if the deficit is bond-financed) or more inflation (if the deficit is financed by printing money). Either result is a GDP growth killer.

In fact, the chronic budget deficits of the United States are largely structural in nature. This bodes exceedingly ill for the long-term success of the fiscal stimulus package that the Obama administration instituted immediately upon taking office. Indeed, one very clear danger is that using such a fiscal policy fix to stimulate the U.S. economy in the presence of a large structural budget deficit ultimately may be a longer-term road to depression and ruin.

In these turbulent economic times, your organization must keep in mind this kind of clear and ever-present danger as it monitors the government spending component of the GDP forecasting equation.

Action Item

Log on to the Dismal Scientist Web site at www.economy.com/dismal/navarro and read the latest U.S. Treasury Budget report. Review the current status of the budget deficit. Consider whether the need to finance that deficit poses a danger to your organization's ability to raise capital. In doing so, try to determine how much of the budget deficit is structural and how much is cyclical in nature.

CHAPTER 12

How Do I Fear Thee, Inflation?
Let Me Count the Ways

When in 1965 [Federal Reserve chairman William McChesney Martin] decided to raise interest rates to try to stave off inflation brought on by the Vietnam War, Lyndon Johnson called Mr. Martin to his ranch in Texas to berate him about the political consequences of a rate rise. Mr. Martin stood firm. The Fed had to "lean against the wind" of inflation, he said. His job, as he famously quipped, was to "take away the punch bowl just when the party gets going."

—The Economist

Like a dark thundercloud, the specter of inflation hangs over the gross domestic product (GDP) forecasting equation as an ever-present reminder that all good economies may eventually come to a recessionary end. In fact, in the pantheon of recessionary triggers, inflation may not be the reigning king, but it is certainly its darkest prince.

Technically, inflation is defined as an upward movement of prices from one year to the next. It is measured by the percentage change in price indices, such as the Consumer Price Index (CPI) and the Producer Price Index (PPI). Paradoxically, while inflation is often an indication of a robust economic expansion, it poses the danger of triggering a recession, either directly or indirectly.

On the direct danger front, inflation negatively affects all three nongovernment components in the GDP equation. Inflation reduces consumption because rising prices pinch consumer budgets and erode purchasing power. Inflation reduces business investment because interest rates invariably rise with inflation, and higher interest rates, in turn, lead to reduced capital expenditures. This is because as the cost of money goes up, projects that would have turned a profit at lower interest rates no longer will do so and are thus canceled. On top of this, inflation even directly reduces exports in the GDP equation by raising export prices and thereby reducing global demand.

On the *indirect* danger front, if inflation rises above the Fed's unofficial target rate—usually around 2%—the Federal Reserve may be motivated to begin a new round of interest rate hikes. Of course, once the Fed starts hiking interest rates, all three of the nongovernment components of the GDP equation are suppressed.

Consumption falls as consumers buy fewer interest-rate-sensitive durable goods, such as autos, appliances, furniture, and houses. Business investment slows because companies reduce their capital expenditures for new plant and equipment. Even exports slow because higher interest rates translate into a stronger dollar as foreign investors are attracted by higher interest rates in the United States. As the dollar strengthens, U.S. exports become more expensive, and U.S. companies sell fewer exports.

That the one-two punch of inflation followed by a round of Fed rate hikes can knock the U.S. economy into a recession is underscored by this startling fact: At least six of the nine recessions since World War II have been preceded by just such a double punch. Exhibit 12.1 graphically illustrates this danger.

You can see clearly in Exhibit 12.1 how inflation, as measured by the black-lined Consumer Price Index core inflation rate, began to accelerate in January 2004. In response, in June 2004, as the core inflation rate approached the Fed's unofficial target of 2%, the Fed then began an extremely aggressive round of rate hikes—as indicated by the gray line charting the intended Fed Funds rate.

Over the next 24 months, the Fed would raise interest rates by fully 425 basis points (4.25%); in the exhibit, you can clearly see

Exhibit 12.1   One-Two Inflation-Rate Hike Punch and the Crash of 2007 to 2009

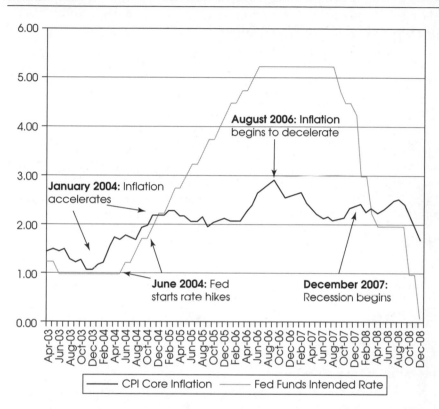

that this anti-inflation medicine worked. In August 2006, as the economy softened—and the housing bubble accelerated its historic collapse—core CPI inflation once again began to decelerate.

Interestingly, despite these and other growing signs of recessionary troubles on the horizon, the Fed was very slow to react to the slowdown. Indeed, the Fed would wait until September 2007—just months before the December onset of the crash—to start cutting interest rates once again. Perhaps never have the phrases first "too much too soon" and then "too little too late" been more appropriate.

Given the Federal Reserve's sad and sordid history in triggering recessions when trying to fight inflation, it is worth understanding the Hobson's choice the Fed faces whenever inflation rears its ugly head—as well as the two types of inflation the Fed must deal with.

JOBS-INFLATION TRADE-OFF

In its mission, the Federal Reserve always faces two very conflicting goals. On one hand, Fed policy must be loose enough to keep almost every voter in the country who wants a job employed. On the other hand, the Fed also must ensure price stability.

That these two goals are often conflicting is embodied in the economist's version of a Hobson's choice known as the Phillips Curve. The Phillips Curve describes an (almost always) iron-clad trade-off between increasing economic growth and increasing inflation. The existence of this trade-off may be traced to at least one kind of inflation known as demand-pull inflation.

Demand-pull inflation comes from too much money chasing too few goods. It is an aptly named inflation because it literally is caused by too much demand in the economy for the goods and services that are available. This type of inflation happens when an economy tries to grow beyond its potential output. In such a case, labor shortages drive up wages, product shortages drive up prices, and up the inflationary spiral goes.

The Federal Reserve invariably responds to such demand-pull inflation by raising interest rates. This is because under the prevailing doctrine of Keynesian economics, the Fed is seen as the front line of defense against inflation. In fact, as humorously highlighted in the opening quotation to this chapter, the Fed's job is to "take away the punch bowl just when the party is getting good."

While the Federal Reserve must raise interest rates to fight inflation, it faces the problem of knowing how high and how fast to raise rates—and when to stop. Historically, we know at least one thing: The Federal Reserve almost never gets it right. Refer back to Exhibit 12.1, and you once again get the picture.

For all these reasons, it is essential that every business executive seeking to become a truly accurate economic forecaster follow the course of inflation in the economy. When you watch inflation, what you really are looking for is for any sign that the Federal Reserve may begin a new cycle of interest rate hikes. Once the Fed begins a new cycle, often it is just a matter of time before a recession ensues.

TAKING THE ECONOMY'S INFLATIONARY PULSE

As for the inflation indicators to watch, the two most important are the Consumer Price Index and the Producer Price Index. The PPI measures inflation at the wholesale level while the CPI measures it at the retail level.

Following the PPI is important because inflation at the wholesale level invariably shows up down the road at the retail level. The Producer Price Index can give you a bit of an early warning that inflation may be brewing. Nevertheless, popularly, the CPI is viewed as the more important of the leading inflation indicators.

COST-PUSH VERSUS DEMAND-PULL INFLATION

Now, before we leave this chapter, there is one very important final point to make about using the inflation data to handicap the possibility of a Fed rate hike. Making this point involves another literacy builder and requires that we learn a little bit about the second type of inflation that can afflict an economy. This type of inflation is known as cost-push inflation.

While demand-pull inflation comes from too much money chasing too few goods, cost-push inflation comes about when the economy suffers from an energy price shock or a food price shock. Here's why this distinction is so important:

> While any increase in demand-pull inflation is likely to increase the chances that the Federal Reserve will *raise* interest rates, any increase in cost-push inflation actually *reduces* the possibility of a Fed rate hike.

The Federal Reserve is less likely to raise interest rates in the presence of cost-push inflation because this type of inflation effectively acts as a tax on the economy. By slowing the economy down all by itself without the need of a rate hike, cost-push inflation effectively does the work of the Fed.

To understand the nature of this cost-push inflation tax, think about what happens when gasoline prices rise at the pump. Your wallet is squeezed, and you have less money to spend on restaurants, shoes, and any number of other things. Moreover, at least some of the money you pay at the pump goes right into the pockets of foreign oil producers—and right out of the U.S. economy. In this way, cost-push inflation acts as a contractionary shock on the economy; and the Federal Reserve would never add to such a contractionary shock by raising interest rates.

Because the emergence of demand-pull versus cost-push inflation has such a very different effect on Fed behavior, it is essential to distinguish between the two when reviewing the inflation data. Fortunately, making this distinction is very easy because the CPI and PPI reports distinguish between so-called core inflation and non-core inflation.

As a general, simplified rule, core inflation represents demand-pull inflation while non-core inflation represents cost-push inflation. And note, the reason why energy and food prices are excluded from core inflation is that they are considered to be highly volatile. While food and oil prices may rapidly go up, they also often rapidly go down.

In summary, follow the inflation indicators as part of your GDP forecasting equation protocol because inflation can trigger a recession both directly and indirectly. And know the difference between demand-pull and cost-push inflation and how the Fed is likely to react to each.

Action Item

Log on to the Dismal Scientist Web site at www.economy.com/dismal/navarro and read the latest reports for the CPI and PPI. Determine whether the inflation rate is rising or falling. If inflation is rising, is the rise due to an increase in core inflation or non-core inflation? Ask yourself if the Federal Reserve is likely to be raising or lowering interest rates.

CHAPTER 13

Why the Bond Market Is not a Casino

Beware the Ides of March—and inverted yield curves.

—Greg Autry

One of the most essential tasks of the Always a Winner manager is to monitor the bond market's yield curve spread regularly. This yield curve spread is one of the most accurate forecasting tools available to you and your executive team. It defines the relationship between the yields on the short-term, 3-month Treasury bill and the long-term, 10-year Treasury note.

In monitoring the yield curve spread, always be on the lookout for a yield curve inversion. This happens whenever the yield on the 3-month T-bill rises above the yield on the 10-year bond, which is called a negative spread. Such inverted yield curves and negative spreads have accurately predicted six of the last seven recessions!

The mighty forecasting power of the yield curve spread is illustrated in Exhibit 13.1. This exhibit graphs the yield curve spread between 1982 and 2008. Any time the graph falls below the zero line in the exhibit, the yield curve spread has turned negative and, as true as the compass points north, it is signaling a recession on the horizon.

Exhibit 13.1   Inverted Yield Curve Signals Recession

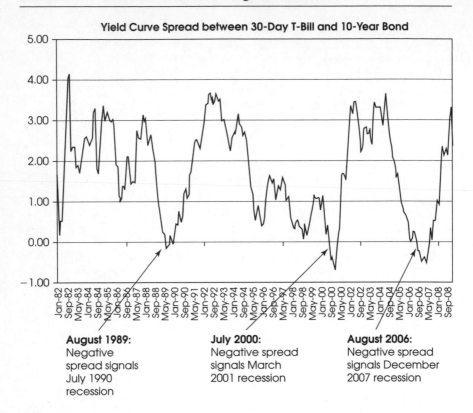

August 1989:
Negative
spread signals
July 1990
recession

July 2000:
Negative spread
signals March
2001 recession

August 2006:
Negative spread
signals December
2007 recession

For example, you can see in Exhibit 13.1 that in foreshadowing the July 1990 to March 1991 recession, the yield curve spread first went negative in August of 1989—almost a year before the recession began.

For the March 2001 recession, the warning sign came eight months before the downturn as the normally positive upward-sloping yield curve spread turned down in July 2000.

Finally, in the case of the crash of 2007 to 2009, the yield curve spread turned negative in August 2006. This was a recessionary warning shot fired a full 16 months before the onset of this crash.

In all cases, observant business executives had plenty of time to prepare for the recessions these yield curve inversions were signaling.

YIELD CURVE PRIMER

Just why does the yield curve normally slope upward, and why is a negative yield curve spread (i.e., an "inverted" yield curve) such an accurate predictor of recession? To answer these two questions, let's first define the term *bond yield* and see how it is calculated.

The yield on any given bond is the return an investor receives when the bond is purchased and held to maturity; and a bond's *yield to maturity* is calculated simply by discounting all future payments by an interest rate, or discount rate, that makes the present value of those payments equal to the current price of the bond.

For example, if you buy a new 10-year bond at its par value of $100 and the interest rate or coupon rate paid on that bond is 10% per year, the bond's initial yield will be 10%—exactly equal to the interest rate paid. Now, if the price of that bond in the market subsequently rises to $110, the coupon rate paid on that bond still remains at 10%, and you, the bond holder, will receive a coupon payment of $10 paid once per year. However, at this new and higher bond price, the bond's effective yield to maturity falls to 8.5%. This is the discount rate at which the present value of those annual $10 coupon payments equal the bond's new price of $110.

Note that this example introduces several technical terms, such as *discounting,* the *discount rate,* and *present value* that assume a basic level of economic literacy. However, even if you are not familiar with these terms, you can understand this: If the price of a bond goes *up* and the interest rate paid on that bond doesn't change, the effective yield of the bond has to *fall* because the bond buyer has paid a higher price for the right to earn the same return. From this example, we see a relationship absolutely critical to understanding how yield curves invert. In particular:

> Bond yields are *inversely* related to bond prices. Thus, if investors drive the price of, say, the long bond up through increased demand, the yield of the long bond will fall.

Now, in the normal situation, the yield curve slopes gently upward, with long-term yields generally 1% to 2% higher than short-term yields. This upward-sloping normal yield curve reflects the concerns that bond holders have about the inflationary risks of holding a bond with a fixed interest rate over a long period of time. That's precisely why, to compensate for these inflationary risks, bond sellers like the U.S. Treasury Department must offer higher interest rates on the long-term bonds they issue.

While the logic of an upward-sloping yield curve is compelling, what doesn't appear to make any sense at all is why any rational bond investor would ever accept a yield on a long-term government bond that is lower than the yield on a short-term Treasury bill. Yet this is precisely the seemingly paradoxical situation that occurs when the yield curve inverts.

To resolve this paradox, and thereby come to understand how the normally upward-sloping yield curve can invert, it is important to understand the two very different forces that determine the ever-changing shape of the yield curve over time. The first force is the Federal Reserve, which moves the short end of the yield curve. The second force is the bond market itself. Through their buying and selling activities, bond investors move the long end of the curve down or up.

TWO FORCES THAT MOVE THE YIELD CURVE

Just how does the Federal Reserve move the short end of the yield curve up or down? It does so by raising or cutting interest rates as it conducts monetary policy to keep the economy on track.

If the Fed wants to stimulate the economy to fight a recession, it cuts short-term interest rates. This moves the short end of the yield curve down. If, however, the Fed wants to fight inflation, it hikes short-term interest rates to curb investment and cool the over-heated economy. This moves the short end of the yield curve up.

At the other end of the yield curve, bond market investors move the long end of the yield curve by either increasing or decreasing their demand for long-term Treasury securities in response to changing economic conditions. For example, if a majority of bond market investors anticipate inflation, they know future interest rates will be higher than today's interest rates. In this case, bond market investors will be *net sellers* of the long bond because they do not want to get locked in to the current, relatively low bond yields that will likely not keep pace with inflation. This net selling, in turn, drives the long end of the yield curve up as bond prices fall.

Now consider the opposite case: If a majority of bond market investors anticipate a decrease in inflation—because of the onset of a recession!—these investors will become *net buyers* of the long bond. They want to lock in today's relatively higher bond yields before recession and deflation reduce interest rates. This net buying activity drives up the long bond's price, and the long end of the yield curve falls.

That this type of behavior among bond investors represents a very intelligent and sophisticated form of speculation is graphically underscored by one of the great bond market speculations of all time. In the late 1970s, inflation was extremely high and interest rates had soared into the double digits. At this time, the Federal Reserve chairman, Paul Volcker, began one of the most aggressive rounds of interest rate hikes in U.S. history. Anticipating an economic crash from these rate hikes, many bond speculators rushed in to buy the long bond.

During the resultant yield curve inversion, short-term yields hit 15% as the Fed kept raising interest rates while the long-term yield was 14%. Of course, any speculator able to lock into this 14% yield by buying the long bond at this point made out like an absolute bandit. Over the next few years, under the weight of recession and deflation, short-term interest rates fell to 5% while long-term yields settled in at around 7%. At this point, as the yield curve resumed its normal shape, holding a portfolio of long bonds with a 14% yield was like robbing a bank—or the Federal Reserve, as the case turned out to be.

TYPICAL YIELD CURVE INVERSION SCENARIO

From this explanation of the two forces that move the yield curve, it should be clear that a yield curve inversion and negative spread comes about when two things happen: The Federal Reserve raises short-term interest rates to fight inflation and a majority of bond investors become net buyers of the long bond because they believe the Fed rate hikes will trigger a recession. In fact, the 2001 recession offers a textbook example of this typical scenario.

In June 1999, the Federal Reserve began a round of interest rate hikes that would eventually raise short-term interest rates by 175 basis points over the next 11 months. The goal of then Fed chairman Alan Greenspan was to engineer a soft landing—the Fed rate hikes would be just enough to gently tamp down on inflationary pressures but not restrictive enough to choke off investment and trigger a recession.

Greenspan's desire for a soft landing notwithstanding, as the Fed kept raising interest rates, it became more and more apparent that Greenspan would overshoot his target. Once bond speculators believed an alternative hard landing was in the offing, they quickly became net buyers of the long bond. Of course, they did so to lock in high yields that would likely be much lower once the recession hit and inflation abated.

It was through this combination of Fed rate hikes and the net buying of the long bond that the yield curve inverted in July 2000—an unlucky 13 months after the cycle of Fed rate hikes had begun. Of course, 8 months later, the economy would succumb to the very recession that bond market speculators had predicted through their net bond-buying behavior.

It should be clear from this discussion that the bond market is decidedly *not* a gambling casino. Rather, the bond market is much more like a very sophisticated forecasting tool. The intelligent speculations of a myriad of very informed investors can reveal the likely direction of the business cycle. Given the yield curve's remarkable accuracy in predicting key recessionary turning points in the U.S. economy over the last 40 years, any business executive who ignores the collective wisdom of the yield curve does so at his or her own peril.

Action Item

Check the current shape of the yield curve at www.bloomberg.com. Go to the link for government bonds, and you will see a picture of the current yield curve and be able to read the latest data for all of the various points along the yield curve. Look carefully at the spread between the 3-month T-bill and the 10-year Treasury note. Is it negative? If you want to see how the yield curve has moved historically over time, check out the highly entertaining and informative living yield curve animation at www.SmartMoney.com.

14

Why Forecasting a Recession Is No Bull (Market)

Like the bond market's yield curve spread, the stock market is a very powerful predictor of business cycle turning points. Indeed, once the stock market establishes a clear downward bearish trend, there is a very high probability that a recession will soon ensue.

The best way to understand why a bear market often signals a recession is to understand what a stock price really reflects. Stripped to its essence, a company's stock price reflects nothing more than an expectation of a future stream of earnings.

In general, the earnings of most companies rise in economic expansions and fall during recessions. Accordingly, any stock market investor who believes the business cycle will be in an expansionary mode is likely to be bullish and buying stocks. If the majority of investment dollars in the stock market reflects this bullish position, the stock market trend will be up on the consensus speculation that the economy will continue in its expansionary mode.

If, however, stock market investors anticipate that a recession is on the horizon, they will begin selling stocks. If enough stock market investors become net sellers, any bullish uptrend will quickly morph into a dangerous bearish downtrend. Any such downtrend may signal concerns that a recession may be on the way—or that a recession in progress may continue for the foreseeable future.

THE STOCK MARKET IS NOT A CASINO

Just how do stock market investors go about their business of anticipating the direction of the business cycle and handicapping the
probability of a recession? The smartest investors with the largest
sums of money who lead the market trend pay very close attention
precisely to the same kinds of key leading indicators and reports we
have examined in this book—from the Economic Cycle Research
Institute Weekly Leading Index, consumer confidence, new home
sales, the Institute for Supply Management Manufacturing Index,
and the Consumer Price Index to the International Trade report,
the U.S. Treasury Budget report, and the yield curve spread.

It follows from these observations that, contrary to one popular
characterization, the stock market is not some giant casino in which
investors are betting recklessly on some meandering random walk.
Rather, like the bond market and its prescient yield curve spread,
the stock market is a very efficient forecasting supercomputer
that runs on the core assumption that stock prices reflect nothing
more—or less—than the expectation of a future stream of earnings
that is contingent on the strength or weakness of the economy.

Exhibit 14.1 illustrates how the onset of a bear market often quite
accurately signals a coming recession. This exhibit charts the progress
of the Standard & Poor's (S&P) 500 index from the beginning of
one of the longest bull markets in history in the early 1990s to the
bearish depths of the crash of 2007 to 2009. The S&P 500 index is
used because it accounts for over 80% of the total market capitalization of the corporations in the United States. As such, it best reflects
the overall stock market.

You can see very clearly in Exhibit 14.1 that the bull market of the
1990s ended with an emphatic exclamation point in August 2000
after which it began a very steep bearish downtrend. This August
2000 stock market top came fully seven months before the onset of
the March 2001 recession and provided a very strong signal of that
coming downturn.

Similarly, in the exhibit you can see the very same process repeat
itself in advance of the crash of 2007 to 2009. After finding a market bottom between September 2002 and March 2003, the S&P 500
resumed a strong upward bullish trend. However, this new bull market would be far shorter than its predecessor. In October 2007—
less than four years later—this new bullish uptrend reached its market

Exhibit 14.1   How Bear Markets Signal Recession

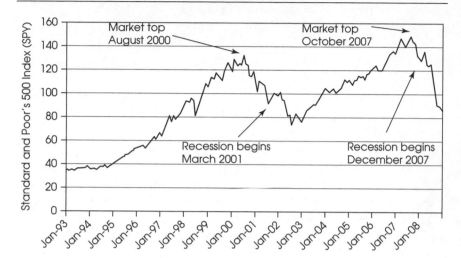

top and promptly established what would become one of the steepest bear market declines in history.

Over the next year, this new bear market would wipe out trillions of dollars of wealth and severely damage the retirement plans of millions of Americans. In doing so, this devastating bear market signaled the onset of the recession in December 2007 several months in advance, thereby validating once again the power of the stock market as a forecasting tool. The steepness of the market's decline also very accurately signaled the severity of economic crash that would be coming.

It should be abundantly clear from the exhibit that together with the bond market's yield curve spread, the stock market provides business executives with extremely important information with which to guide their companies through an up-and-down economy. Accordingly, any executive who ignores the messages of the stock and bond markets is just plain foolish.

ASSESSING THE STOCK MARKET'S TREND

One way to assess the stock market's bullish and bearish trends is simply to keep a daily eye on the movement of the Standard & Poor's 500 index—the best broad-based measure of stock market activity in the world. This, however, is a very passive approach to a critical task of the Master Cyclist executive.

Indeed, simply sitting on the sidelines and watching the stock market is far too staid an approach to fully engage a busy executive's competitive spirit and cognitive prowess. That's why I strongly recommend a much more active approach to every business executive and MBA student I come into contact with. It involves trading a $1 million mock stock portfolio as a forecasting tool, and it takes no more than a few minutes a week.

To conduct this forecasting exercise, simply go to a Web site such as www.stocktrak.com and sign up for a mock trading account with a value of $1 million. Once you have set up your account, your Master Cyclist forecasting task is to trade a portfolio once a week that contains only one stock: the exchange-traded fund for the Standard & Poor's 500 index that was used to track the market's movements in Exhibit 14.1.

The stock symbol for the Standard & Poor's 500 exchange-traded fund is SPY. Here is your specific mission: On a weekly basis, you must put all the money in your portfolio into SPY in either a long or a short position.

You will buy, or go long, the S&P 500 if your analysis of the economy using the GDP equation and our other forecasting tools leads you to believe that the economy will continue in expansionary mode. If, however, new economic information has come along to indicate that a recession may soon be on the horizon, you should take a short position in the exchange-traded fund. By short-selling SPY, your portfolio will increase in value *only* if the stock market goes down.

Now, here's the beauty of this stock market simulation. It helps act as a very important system of checks and balances on the other forecasting tools you will be using to recession-proof your organization. Specifically, if you begin losing significant sums of money on your weekly speculations about the direction of the stock market, there is a very good chance that your speculation about the direction of the business cycle is very wrong. If, the value of your portfolio is growing, however, chances are that your expectations about the direction of the business cycle are going to be right on and you are going to be making the right strategic and tactical decisions to manage the business cycle.

If you are a top-level executive in a very big company, please do not think this exercise is beneath you or not worth the few minutes of time it requires each week. When push comes to shove, it is an exercise that forces you, on a weekly basis, to confront what may soon be your recessionary demons. Plus, if you perform this exercise well, you will never suffer the kind of heavy stock market losses that so many people sustained in the stock market crash of 2007 to 2009. Instead, you will be constantly honing your economic and financial market literacy in a way that will pay big dividends, both for your company and for your own personal retirement portfolio.

Why a Bear Market May Be a Self-Fulfilling Forecasting Prophecy

While the stock market is a leading indicator of the business cycle, once a downward market trend signals a possible recession, such a downturn can, in and of itself, often ensure that a recession actually occurs. To see why, consider what happens when billions or even trillions of dollars of stock market wealth simply vanish for investors when stock prices head sharply down.

In this situation, investors' net worth shrinks dramatically. This, in turn, cuts sharply into their ability to borrow against their assets in order to fund other investments. This situation can lead to reductions in the investment component of the GDP equation.

At the same time, a large loss in stock market wealth can trigger a negative wealth effect that manifests as reduced consumption. This occurs because every time investors look at their declining portfolios, they choose to spend a lot less.

In fact, many investors can become outright depressed in bear markets. Research studies actually have shown that the mental impact of a stock loss is three times stronger than the high investors experience on a stock price gain.

With both investment and consumption falling in reaction to a falling stock market, the economy slows further—and recession may indeed ensue.

Action Item

Go to www.stocktrak.com and sign up for a mock trading account with a value of $1 million. Start the forecasting exercise described in this chapter.

CHAPTER 15

How the Corporate Earnings Calendar Literally "Guides" Your Strategy

With Alcoa's earnings report on Tuesday, corporate America will start filling in the blanks on one of the most uncertain quarters in years. Alcoa, which traditionally goes first each earnings' season, starts the rush of firms reporting their July through September sales and profits.

For some market participants, the aluminum giant is a bellwether and early sign of third-quarter trends.... It's a key time for the U.S. economy, as it is threatened by the summer's market turmoil and the decline of the housing sector. Alcoa sells a lot of aluminum to U.S. home builders, and it is exposed to other broad swaths of the economy, including durable goods and the troubled auto makers.
—"Alcoa Kicks Off an Uneasy Earnings Season," *Business Week*

Like clockwork, every quarter on Wall Street, the earnings season rolls around; and during this season, every publicly traded corporation must publish a quarterly earnings statement. For stock market investors interested in individual companies, the earnings season provides a wealth of information.

From a business cycle forecasting perspective, the corporate earnings season may be even more important. Collectively, the earnings statements of the myriad reporting companies help paint a very useful picture of the current state of the economy as well as its future direction. In this sense, the earnings season represents an exercise in connecting the individual earnings statement "dots" to discern the broader business cycle picture.

In using the corporate earnings season as a forecasting tool, there are two important questions to ask:

1. Did the majority of the companies, particularly the so-called bellwether companies like Alcoa in the quotation leading off this chapter, meet, miss, or exceed their earnings targets?
2. Did the majority of firms "guide" their forecasts higher or lower, or leave their guidance unchanged? (The term *guidance* refers to the fact that most companies also provide in their earnings announcements whether they expect next-quarter earnings to be above or below the levels previously forecast.)

Of these two questions, the first, related to actual earnings, is slightly less important than the second, about guidance, because the vast majority of companies purposely try to understate their earnings estimates. That way, if these companies can beat their earnings estimates, they usually can get a nice upward pop for their stock price. That said, on the downside, if the majority of companies miss their earnings estimates in any given quarter, that's usually a very strong sign that recessionary troubles may be on the way— or that the economy is already in a recession.

The second question about future earnings guidance is really where the hard truth rubber meets the business cycle forecasting road. If a company guides lower, it is revising its expected earnings for the next one or more quarters downward. In contrast, if a company guides higher, it expects more robust growth in the quarters ahead than it previously forecast.

It is precisely because a firm's guidance reflects its own internal forecasting efforts that the guidance statements issued during the earnings season collectively represent a very powerful signal about the future direction of the economy. If the majority of firms are guiding lower, that is a very strong sign that a recession may be on the way. Conversely, if the majority of firms are guiding higher, that's usually pretty compelling evidence that a recovery may be on the way—or that an economic expansion may be accelerating its rate of growth. Thus, the guidance statements issued during the earnings season will help you guide your own business cycle management strategy.

Note that following the earnings calendar is hardly just an American ritual. This news excerpt from India's largest online business magazine about stock market reaction to an announcement of lowered guidance by one of the Indian economy's most important companies—Infosys— illustrates how the corporate earnings calendar guides both investors and business executives around the world:

> Lower than expected revenue guidance from Infosys is all it took to send the [stock market] indices crashing to their largest single day fall since May of last year. [T]he indices opened deep in the red and steadily lost further ground except for a brief period before noon, when they tried to stabilise. Overall weakness in other Asian markets added to the gloom as technology stocks were hammered down.[1]

FOLLOW THE BELLWETHER COMPANIES

In following the corporate earnings calendar, it is neither necessary nor even desirable for you and your executive team to study the earnings statements and guidance of all of the thousands upon thousands of corporations reporting. Instead, all you need really do is follow a much smaller list of so-called bellwether companies.

Before its downfall as the world's leading carmaker, General Motors was *the* most important American economic bellwether. In fact, it used to be said "What's good for GM is good for America." Today, despite also having been severely weakened in recent years, General Electric (GE) remains an important bellwether. As one of the largest and most broadly diversified companies, GE represents one of the best reflections of overall activity. So, too, however, does the Internet giant Google.

While you may find it surprising that a mere Internet company can rise to the level of an economy-wide bellwether, consider what the Web site 247WallSt.com had to say about the pervasive role that Google now plays:

Google has changed a great deal in the last two years. It is not just the bigger revenue and the growing share of market. It is not that the company has desktop software to compete with Microsoft or that the company owns video sharing giant YouTube. The difference is that Google now has such a large piece of the US internet ad market that it has become a proxy for the overall economy in a way that the car industry was four decades ago.... What this means is that Google's earnings for this quarter will be as good a proxy for the overall economy as the numbers that any company reports this earnings season.[2]

Beyond GE and Google, two other important general business cycle bellwethers include United Parcel Service and Federal Express. Together, these two companies offer important signals about the economy because if parcels and packages are not flowing through these critical delivery service providers, chances are the economy has headed south.

In addition, individual sector bellwethers are also well worth following. My favorite list includes DuPont and the Alcoa to monitor the pulse of heavy industry; Intel, Microsoft, and Nokia to keep an eye on the tech sector; and PepsiCo and Procter & Gamble for some insight into the consumer.

In following the earnings season for your own forecasting purposes, my strong suggestion is that you and your executive team develop your own set of bellwether companies based on the segment or sector of the economy that your company operates in. This will help you better use the earnings calendar data to forecast not just broad economic trends but also your own industry trends.

THE STOCK MARKET AND THE EARNINGS SEASON

The stock market took a sudden dive on Friday after Dow component General Electric reported first quarter earnings before the opening bell. Analysts expected certain divisions such as appliances to be down. What they weren't expecting was weakness across most of their businesses.

— Wall Street Weather

This online news excerpt not only reinforces the point that conclusions about the direction of the business cycle can be inferred from the fate of bellwether companies like GE. It also helps explain why the stock market is a leading indicator of the business cycle.

In this particular case, disappointing earnings from just one single company, GE, caused the entire stock market to decline. This happened because investors interpreted the fall in GE earnings as a strong predictor of a more general fall in corporate earnings and therefore a strong recessionary signal.

If, more broadly, the majority of earnings statements report lower-than-expected earnings and lowered guidance, the almost certain net effect will be to move the stock market in a decidedly downward bearish trend—with the market then signaling a slowdown or recession. In this way, following the stock market as a leading indicator and paying close attention to the corporate earnings season work hand in glove as important forecasting tools.

Action Item

Compile your own list of bellwether companies to follow during the earnings season. Visit a Web site like www.moneycentral.msn.com and find the earnings calendar link under market statistics.[3] During the next earnings season, handicap the prospects of a recession or economic expansion based on the earnings and guidance news of your bellwethers.

STEP II

ALWAYS A WINNER STRATEGIES THROUGH THE BUSINESS CYCLE SEASONS

CHAPTER 16

How to Recession-Proof Your Supply Chain

Now that we have finished Step One in the Always a Winner management process and you have learned to become your own economic forecaster, it's time to put your ability to anticipate movements and key turning points in the business cycle to work. That's where Step Two comes into play.

In Step Two, we learn how to implement a very powerful set of strategies at key points in the business cycle. These are illustrated in Exhibit 16.1.

This exhibit, which was previously introduced in Chapter 4, groups each of the major Always a Winner strategies according to their specific functional activities. These activities include:

1. Production, inventory, and supply chain management
2. Human resources management
3. Advertising and marketing
4. Pricing and credit management
5. Capital expenditures
6. Acquisitions and divestitures
7. Capital financing

In the remainder of this chapter, we focus on the first critical functional area: production, inventory, and supply chain management. Then, in the next six chapters, we examine each of the remaining functional areas in more detail.

Exhibit 16.1 Always a Winner Strategies over the Business Cycle

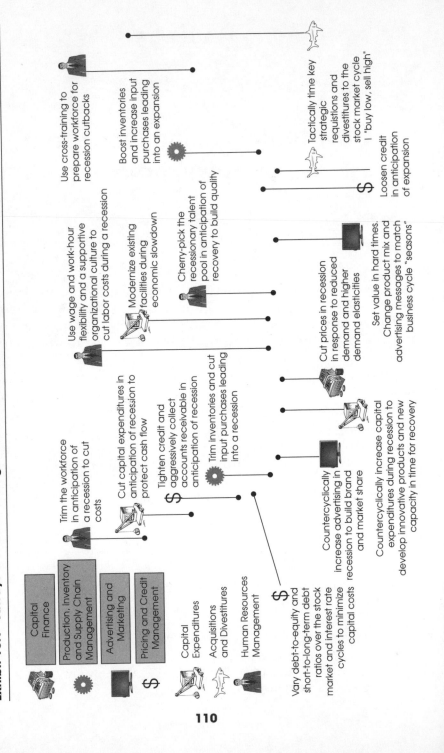

Capital Finance

Production, Inventory and Supply Chain Management

Advertising and Marketing

Pricing and Credit Management

Capital Expenditures

Acquisitions and Divestitures

Human Resources Management

Vary debt-to-equity and short-to-long-term debt ratios over the stock market and interest rate cycles to minimize capital costs

Trim the workforce in anticipation of a recession to cut costs

Cut capital expenditures in anticipation of recession to protect cash flow

Tighten credit and aggressively collect accounts receivable in anticipation of recession

Trim inventories and cut input purchases leading into a recession

Countercyclically increase advertising in recession to build brand and market share

Countercyclically increase capital expenditures during recession to develop innovative products and new capacity in time for recovery

Use cross-training to prepare workforce for recession cutbacks

Boost inventories and increase input purchases leading into an expansion

Use wage and work-hour flexibility and a supportive organizational culture to cut labor costs during a recession

Modernize existing facilities during economic slowdown

Cherry-pick the recessionary talent pool in anticipation of recovery to build quality

Cut prices in recession in response to reduced demand and higher demand elasticities

Set value in hard times. Change product mix and advertising messages to match business cycle "seasons"

Tactically time key strategic requisitions and divestitures to the stock market cycle I "buy low, sell high"

Loosen credit in anticipation of expansion

DON'T GET LEFT HOLDING THE INVENTORY BAG

Historically, the buildup of large inventories has been the classic sign of a recession and a collateral symptom of the collective failure of the corporate world to anticipate its onset. Of course, once inventories begin to build in the early stages of an economic slowdown, companies inevitably begin to cut production and lay people off. This contributes further to weakening the economy, leads to an even larger inventory surplus, and serves only to deepen the recession.

AMD Bloats Its Inventories

One company that always seems to be a player in this sad little business cycle saga is chip maker Advanced Micro Devices (AMD)— the perennial number two to market leader Intel. One of the big reasons AMD has perennially chased the tailpipe of Intel is the Reactive Cyclist nature of its organization. From mismanaging its inventories and overpaying for strategic acquisitions to mistiming its capital expenditures, AMD can always be counted on to screw it up whenever the business cycle turns down.

Consider AMD's inventory mismanagement during the crash of 2007–2009. In the fourth quarter of 2007, on the eve of that crash, AMD was holding about 76 days of outstanding inventory. At this point, and in typical AMD fashion, the company's executive team ignored the many growing signs of the impending recession and instead clung to its own highly optimistic forecast for its vaunted new quad-core processors. On the basis of that forecast, AMD actually began to ramp up production for these processors just as the recession began in December 2007. Said AMD's chief executive officer (CEO) in its 2007 annual report: "In 2008, we plan to deliver quad-core processors in significant volumes to the server and desktop markets."

As it would turn out, producing those quad processors was one thing. But getting anyone to take delivery of large numbers of them was quite another. In fact, over the course of the next year, AMD's inventory would increase from 76 days in December 2007 to 90 days by December 2008.[1] Of course, as the heavy hammer of the recession came down on the chip industry, AMD was confronted with the worst case Reactive Cyclist scenario: a huge inventory write-down.

Within a year of AMD's CEO promising to ramp up production, the company had to report a whopping $227 million inventory impairment charge. Over this period, while tech stocks were falling by 42%, AMD's stock fell nearly 71% and all the way down to near-penny-stock territory.

The tragedy here is that had AMD even kept its days of inventory outstanding at its December 2007 levels, it would have conserved $134 million in cash. Like a typical Reactive Cyclist, however, AMD saw an opportunity for growth based on its new technology but failed to factor in the emerging recessionary reality that the economy wouldn't support the level of inventory being produced. In fact, as late as March 2008, AMD's CEO appeared to remain utterly clueless to the disaster about to engulf his company. Here's what he had to say in his annual letter to shareholders:

> As we enter 2008, you [shareholders] and our customers are not alone in having great expectations of AMD. We have great expectations of ourselves and I have enormous confidence that those expectations will not go unmet in the years to come.

Saks's "Feel Good" CEO Doesn't Feel So Good Anymore

If there was an award for the worst inventory management leading into the crash of 2007 to 2009, the luxury department store Saks Fifth Avenue would give even the clueless AMD a run for its money. In February 2008, even as the recession was already well under way, Saks CEO Steve Sadove sent his merchandisers jetting off to Milan and Paris to place orders for upcoming holiday season *at the same levels as the previous year.*

Interestingly, while Saks CEO Steve Sadove knew other retailers were starting to suffer, he falsely assumed that Saks would be immune from the slowdown because, as he saw it, "our customer feels good."[2] In fact, it wasn't until almost a year into the recession, in September 2008, when Sadove saw the Dow Jones average drop almost 800 points that he realized there were problems.

Stuck by then with a huge inventory overhang, Sadove panicked and proceeded to shatter a huge industry taboo. Specifically, he instituted steep discounts of up to 70% well before the holiday season had even begun in earnest.

The cascading effect in the industry was brutal as other department stores like Neiman Marcus and Barneys had to discount to compete, many smaller boutiques went bankrupt, and

Saks's performance metrics suffered mightily. As noted in the *New York Times:*

> For the three months that ended Jan. 31, 2009, Saks lost $98.75 million, or 72 cents a share, compared with a profit of $39.47 million, or 26 cents a share, a year ago. . . . [A]s if the consumer spending shutdown were not enough, Saks's credit ratings have been downgraded, and its profit margins have eroded.[3]

For the longer term, Saks really shot itself in the head rather than in its foot. In the wake of Saks's deep discounting, customers are now questioning the entire premise of luxury goods that Saks is founded on.

Of course, the most darkly comic aspect of this whole episode has to be two Yin and Yang utterances by Sadove almost a year apart: When he sent his merchandisers off to Milan and Paris to load up on inventory, he justified the trip by stating that "our customer feels good." Once the luxury goods hit the fan, Sadove would then have to confess to a group of investors and analysts: "If I were to look at it on a profitability basis, I don't feel good at all."

TRIM INVENTORIES IN ANTICIPATION OF RECESSIONS

Of course, Master Cyclist organizations want no part of the kind of vicious cycle experienced by the likes of AMD and Saks. That's why, in anticipation of a recession, Master Cyclists begin not only to cut production and inventory. They also cut their purchases and stockpiling of whatever raw materials, components, and other production inputs they might need for their factories and facilities. A case in point on the opposite end of the pole from AMD involves the Potash Corporation of Saskatchewan Canada.

Potash Prepares for the Worst

> *To prepare for growth, we continue to build our potash capacity. . . . As we have in the past, we will bring on this capacity when it is needed, remaining true to our long-held strategy of matching production to market demand. . . . We will not push our products in the markets when there is a lull, but we will be prepared as demand growth returns.*
> —William J. Doyle, President and Chief Executive,
> 2008 Annual Report

Potash is an integrated fertilizer and feed products company that operates mines in Canada and plant facilities for the production of fertilizer-related products, such as nitrogen, ammonia, urea, and phosphate.

Recognizing the bubblelike nature of the economy and seeing the recessionary handwriting on the wall, Potash's executive team presciently began to cut both its inventory and factor input purchases even as it began to cut production at its Canadian mining operations. Anticipating greater volatility in the bubble economy, Potash also made a very significant investment in a forecasting and supply chain management system that, in effect, now acts as a far more efficient early-warning system of any impending weakening of demand.

As a result of strategic actions such as these, Potash not only weathered the 2007 to 2009 storm; it has prospered.

COURAGE TO GO AGAINST THE HERD

Of course, it can be very difficult to begin cutting production and curtailing the purchase of factor inputs in the late stages of an economic expansion, as Potash's executive team did when times were still good. However, the courage to make such cuts is what separates the strategic business cycle manager from the Reactive Cyclist herd.

In making such production cuts, the Master Cyclist executive team is always seeking to balance the costs of holding inventory versus the costs of not having enough inventory on hand—so-called stock-out costs. In this regard, as a recession looms, the downside risks of holding too much inventory quickly overtake the rewards of having enough products on hand for distribution and sale.

It's not just the bottom recessionary part of the business cycle that the Master Cyclist worries about in managing the supply chain. The Master Cyclist also understands that:

It is equally important to ramp up production and begin building inventories during a recession as soon as a recovery appears to be on the horizon. In this way, the Master Cyclist will be first to market with the most innovative goods that it is able to produce.

This observation underscores one of the most subtle but important functions of trimming inventories in anticipation of a recession. Organizations that fail to do so are often stuck with products that are either technologically obsolete and/or out of fashion. In such cases, these inventories either must be written off as losses during the recession or sold at steep discounts after the economy recovers.

This problem of "technology fade" in high-tech sectors with relatively short product cycles underscores the critical importance of learning to become a Master Cyclist. Sadly, as AMD found out, a warehouse full of last year's microprocessors is worth considerably less than, shall we say, an inventory overhang of fertilizer for a company like Potash.

The broader point is that more nimble Master Cyclists unencumbered with inventory overhangs can put newer and better products on shelves as soon as they once again ramp up production to greet the new expansion.

BUILD-TO-ORDER CUTS INVENTORY COSTS

At Centex, we have been consistent in our actions based on the current market realities . . . to effectively navigate this unprecedented cycle.

—Timothy Eller, CEO, Centex

While cutting inventories in anticipation of the recession and building inventories in anticipation of an expansion represents the bread and butter of Master Cyclist inventory management strategies, one other way to strategically manage one's inventories is to essentially not hold any. That's where a build-to-order strategy can come into play.

Consider, for example, America's largest homebuilder, Centex. In the wake of the bursting of the housing bubble and during the crash of 2007 to 2009, Centex moved to a build-to-order production model that substantially reduced its risk of being stuck with expensive unsold inventory. By making this move, Centex was able to improve its gross margins in 2008 while reducing sales discounts and incentives. As Centex chief financial officer Cathy Smith noted in the company's third quarter earnings call:

Our home building operations were cash flow positive for the fifth straight quarter. This reflects our keen focus on cash and the progressive changes in our business processes. . . . What's more exciting, because of the longer term implications, we are becoming more asset efficient and more profitable as we have almost fully completed our transition to a build-to-order production model. . . . [E]ven at these depressed levels of sales and closings, we can produce positive cash flow.

This was, of course, a time when most other homebuilders were on the ropes.

WILLIAMS-SONOMA SQUEEZES THE SUPPLY CHAIN

Recessions often provide excellent Darwinian opportunities for an organization, as a final strategic move, to cut its supply chain costs by squeezing suppliers. As Pat Connolly, a top executive at the premier specialty home furnishings retailer Williams-Sonoma, has noted: "Being a strong company in a weak environment presents significant opportunities."[4]

In Darwinian fashion, during the crash of 2007 to 2009, Williams-Sonoma successfully renegotiated many of its supply contracts to more favorable terms as its weaker rivals had to cut orders with their suppliers. The performance result included not only lower supply chain costs but also more timely deliveries.[5] As Charles Darwin long ago observed:

In the struggle for survival, the fittest win out at the expense of their rivals because they succeed in adapting themselves best to their environment.

Action Item

Evaluate your organization's performance in its inventory and production management over the last two recessions. Did your organization have to write down large amounts of inventory? And what kind of mechanisms do you use to protect your organization against unwanted inventory buildups? Would a build-to-order model be feasible?

CHAPTER 17

Why Cherry Picking the Talent Pool During Recessions Is Your Quality Key

By engaging in bargain hunting during downturns and hiring talent that would probably not be available during upturns, a company may gain a critical edge over its competitors.
— Professors Charles Greer and Timothy Ireland

This wonderfully insightful strategic advice about cherry picking the recessionary labor pool from an article in the prestigious *Academy of Management Review*[1] serves as the cornerstone of Master Cyclist human resources (HR) management best practices. The real tragedy is that far too many organizations ritually ignore this advice. Here is an all-too-typical scenario:

Oblivious to any increasing signs of an economic downturn in the irrationally exuberant booming good times, a company continues to hire new staff right into the late stages of an economic expansion when wage pressures are highest. When the recession hits, this very same company, now bloated with excess labor costs, is forced into dramatic layoffs. Often some of the company's very best employees wind up being kicked to the curb—and many will be lost forever, often to competitors.

DON'T OVERHIRE AT PREMIUM WAGES LATE INTO AN EXPANSION!

A poster child for exuberantly overhiring and then desperately firing is offered up by the incredibly myopic behavior of the Internet services company Yahoo! during the crash of 2007 to 2009.

Yahoo! Bloats, Then Burns, Its Labor Force

Yahoo! on Wednesday began dropping the axe on employees, following through on a promise to cut its workforce by at least 10 percent in an effort to right its financially listing ship.

As Yahoo! began its second round of layoffs this year, an investment firm, Ivory Investment Management, which owns a 1.5 percent stake in Yahoo!, urged the firm's board to sell its Internet search business to software giant Microsoft.

—AFP News

Yahoo!'s labor meltdown began in typical Reactive Cyclist fashion as the company continued to hire aggressively at premium wages leading right into the very teeth of the 2007 to 2009 crash. In fact, in the two years leading up to that crash, Yahoo! increased its workforce by almost 50% while paying premium wages. Of course, once the recession hit, Yahoo! had to lay off many of these very same workers. As the company tried to slash its bloated labor costs, it merely succeeded in crushing morale. As the *New York Times* noted:

"They really, really mishandled this thing," said a manager who was laid off today. "That has a really bad effect on morale, and even the people who are left have a feeling things are really coming apart. It damaged the morale of otherwise good people they want to hang onto."[2]

The Master Cyclist executive team not only avoids this recessionary trap and any attendant mass layoffs and blows to morale. It uses the deepest and darkest days of a recession to cherry pick the very best new hires for its company from a talent pool now swollen with some of the very best and brightest laid off talent from the industry. In this way, this well-timed strategic business cycle management strategy exploits recessions to improve the quality of the organization.

Microsoft Acquires Yahoo!—on the Cherry-Picking Cheap!

An excellent example of such cherry picking is offered up by Microsoft's rapid response to Yahoo!'s mass layoffs and plunging morale. In one brilliant move, Microsoft hired Qi Lu, a former top Yahoo! search and marketing executive and pioneer in search engine technology. He wound up as the president of Microsoft's Online Services. Other prizes included such top-flight execs as Larry Heck and Sean Suchter.

Surely these moves put a huge Cheshire grin on the face of Microsoft chief executive officer Steve Ballmer—whose attempts to acquire Yahoo! had been repeatedly spurned by his seemingly clueless CEO counterpart Jerry Yang. Through this strategic cherry picking, Microsoft was able to acquire some of Yahoo!'s and Yang's best assets without actually having to pay a premium price for the company. Quipped one blogger on Lu's hiring:

> Microsoft's hiring of Lu gives it a 10-year veteran of the company where he did things like lead all of engineering for Yahoo! search and advertising. One would have to assume Microsoft got him for less than the $44.6 billion it offered [to acquire] Yahoo!.

Avon Always Rings Twice During Recessions

While Microsoft performed admirably in the HR dimension during the crash of 2007 to 2009, one of the most astute cherry pickers of all times is the Avon company. In a move worth saluting, Avon cherry picked on a grand scale during the 2001 recession.

As the economy headed south in 2001, Avon's executive team realized that this recession would result in "an ever larger pool of women"[3] to recruit to sell its cosmetics, perfumes, and other products. Avon's executive team also understood quite well that a recession was a great time to sell its products because during these tough times, many women would not be able to "afford department store creams."[4]

To bring this talent into the company, Avon revitalized an old program called Sales Leadership in which the company's top performers are taught how to recruit, train, and supervise their own group of representatives. This program, coupled with a number of other equally aggressive initiatives, allowed Avon to expand its workforce by almost one third—or by roughly one million.[5]

This bold countercyclical hiring strategy had a very dramatic effect on Avon's performance over the next several years. On the strength of record profits, Avon's stock price rose by 16% in 2002 and another 25% in 2003 while sales rose dramatically.

Credit Suisse Cleans Up from Lehman's Mess

When Lehman went bankrupt, the recruitment world went into overdrive.
                              —Jason Kennedy, CEO, Kennedy Associates

This observation by the CEO of a leading executive search firm underscores the tremendous opportunity that a tragedy like the Lehman bankruptcy during 2008 can offer to other members of an industry—even as it underscores the importance of having a strong enough balance sheet to make such a move.

One such company that executed an excellent cherry-picking strategy in the wake of the Lehman bankruptcy was Credit Suisse. It immediately scooped up a significant number of Lehman's top employees—including ex–chief financial officer Erin Callan to run its global hedge fund, Stuart Upcraft as a mergers and acquisitions specialist, Bob Elfring for investment banking, and Robert Pearlman as a managing director for its private banking U.S. unit, just to name a few.

PROTECTING THE WORKFORCE IN TROUBLED TIMES

We prefer to keep our people together to withstand the crisis rather than making deep job cuts in a knee-jerk decision.
                              —David Sun, Chairman, Ernst and Young China

This quotation highlights the fact that it is not just HR strategies that make a Master Cyclist. A Master Cyclist is more broadly a supportive organizational culture that is highly attuned to the business cycle and the need to protect the organization's workforce when bad times come.

At the heart of avoiding layoffs is a recognition among Master Cyclist executive teams that job insecurity kills morale and leads to higher employee turnover in good times. After all, if a company won't protect you in bad times, there is no reason to be loyal to it in good times. Just ask all those employees kicked to the curb by Yahoo! during the crash of 2007 to 2009 crash.

To avoid these morale and turnover issues, the Master Cyclist executive team will surgically use tools in down times, ranging from telecommuting, flexible scheduling, employee sharing, cross-training, and modernizing facilities, to early retirement and educational sabbatical programs.

Early retirement packages in particular can be very appealing to employees, especially when juxtaposed against the far harsher alternative of simply being fired near retirement. While the costs of early retirement programs may be slightly higher, the benefit the company gains in boosting employee morale and loyalty are likely to more than offset all of these costs.

From AFLAC to Rocklin, California

One company that astutely uses a combination of telecommuting, flexible scheduling, employee sharing, and cross-training to help maintain a no-layoff policy is AFLAC, the insurance company that has famously ridden a comedic quacking duck to industry prominence. These types of HR strategics are not just for for-profit companies, however. They can work for local, state, and federal government agencies and nonprofit entities as well.

Consider how the city of Rocklin, California, 25 miles northeast of Sacramento, sought to weather the storm in 2007 to 2009. Like many cities in California, Rocklin struggled in the aftermath of the real estate bubble and the resulting loss of tax revenues. But unlike many California cities, Rocklin was far better prepared.

As the crash approached, Rocklin officials began a series of defensive measures aimed at insulating the city from the approaching storm. It preemptively reduced its budget by making across-the-board cuts. In the HR dimension, as staff members left, the city simply and strategically chose not to replace them. As the recession ensued, City Manager Carlos Urrutia also emulated the same kind of "share the pain" organizational culture of a company like Nucor (see Chapter 26) by recommending classic Master Cyclist techniques, such as retirement incentives and possible furloughs, to avoid layoffs.

Infosys Kills Two Birds with One Sabbatical

As an additional HR Master Cyclist tool, educational sabbaticals at reduced wages can be a great way to increase the skills and capabilities of your employees while likewise boosting morale, increasing loyalty, and trimming labor costs. In fact, many employees, particularly in the middle and upper executive ranks, can benefit from a break in the action, which allows them to return to a business school or some other educational facility. These employees recharge their batteries, energize their brains, and come back to work with exactly the kind of vitality that organizations are going to need once business is booming again.

An excellent example of a high-tech company that has used sabbaticals to protect its high skilled workforce is that of Infosys, India's second largest information technology services provider. During the crash of 2007 to 2009, Infosys offered any employees who had worked for the company for at least two years the opportunity to take a one-year sabbatical to engage in philanthropic activities. Any employees who took advantage of this offer were paid 50% of their salary.

In fact, this approach killed two birds with one sabbatical. It not only helped Infosys retain its employees. It also helped to burnish the image of the company by highlighting its public-interested goals. Such image boosting is particularly important in a country like India, where the poor are exhibiting growing resentment of the wealth accumulation of a new generation of high-technology workers.

AVOID THE FREEZE

[F]reezes have a direct impact because, during a freeze, even if a "Michael Jordan" walks in the door, you would have to send him away! It makes no sense.

—Professor John Sullivan

This observation from Professor Sullivan's Web site offers one last Master Cyclist spin on HR management during a recession. The problem Sullivan identifies is that during a sharp downturn, one of the most damaging, knee-jerk actions a reactive CEO can engage in is the hiring freeze. This classic bad move is a favorite of the emotion-driven executive who wishes to highlight the significance of the threat to the company during the hard times while sending a signal about his or her dedication to preserving the positions of current employees.

These good intentions notwithstanding, the hiring freeze is a double whammy of bad HR strategy. Such a freeze not only prevents managers from recruiting great talent, as Sullivan notes. It also prevents the company from using a downturn to get rid of the deadweight!

The well-known problem here is that once managers realize they won't be able to replace even the worst members of the team, they tend to hang on to underperforming employees they might otherwise jettison. In this way, a hiring freeze often prolongs the job life of incompetents who might not otherwise survive their probationary period. In this way, a "temporary" freeze can have very long-lasting effects.

Even more pernicious, the best employees of an organization will see a freeze announcement as their cue to start printing resumes on a company laser printer—and the best managers will be right behind them. Such an exodus occurs because, during a hiring freeze, departmental and project managers are unlikely to receive adequate resources to perform. In a domino effect, great new endeavors wither and die from lack of resources, bad products are frozen in place, and many of an organization's very best staff are misallocated to efforts that will never prosper.

For all these reasons, a hiring freeze *always* erodes morale, reduces staff quality, kills company flexibility when it is needed most, and signals panic to all of the company's stakeholders. Accordingly, a CEO who "freezes" during a downturn is the last person who should be piloting your organization through recessionary turbulence.

The bottom line: Anytime your company engages in mass layoffs in a recession, you have done something horribly wrong in terms of managing the business cycle. You have either bloated your workforce during the late stages of the economic expansion at high wages and then been forced to slash that workforce, or you have failed to build an organizational culture and institute business cycle–sensitive programs that would have allowed you to avoid this disaster.

Action Item

Carefully review your organization's human resources management policies to determine how closely they conform to Master Cyclist HR principles. Work through this checklist:

- Does your organization countercyclically hire during recessions to build workforce quality—or engage in widespread layoffs whenever times get tough?
- Does your organization have programs such as cross-training and educational sabbaticals to protect its workers?
  Does your organization use slow economic times to modernize and refurbish its facilities?
- Is your organizational culture supportive of sound HR practices?

18

Why Countercyclical Advertising Is the Best Way to Build Brand and Market Share

Advertise! And better yet, advertise a lot. Why? Because there is ample evidence to support the fact that maintaining or increasing your advertising and marketing investment in slow [economic] times is actually more effective than in . . . growth periods. A key reason is that when the marketing and advertising "noise" goes down, the voices of those still talking sound that much louder.
—John Kypriotakis, Lysis International

Whehen a recession comes, it is often the marketing department that gets the very first knock on the door from stern-faced bean counters carrying an edict to cut costs. Inevitably, when a firm slashes its advertising during a recession, it merely succeeds in cutting off its nose to spite its face.

Kmart's bean-counting chief executive officer (CEO) Chuck Conway learned this iron law of strategic business cycle management the very hardest of ways. In the 2001 recession, Conway slashed Kmart's advertising budget in a pennywise fashion that opened the door to an absolute pounding by Wal-Mart. While Kmart cut deeply, Wal-Mart significantly upped its advertising. While Kmart's sales revenue plummeted, Wal-Mart revenues increased. While Kmart went into bankruptcy, Wal-Mart boosted its market share. As Conway would later admit, "There is no doubt we made a mistake by cutting too much advertising too fast."[1]

ADVERTISE IN RECESSIONS, BUILD MARKET SHARE

In fact, recessions are the best time to increase your advertising for at least two reasons.

1. Advertising levels are generally down so there is far less congestion in the advertising market. This allows your advertising messages to be heard far more clearly and far more sharply—particularly if your rivals are in full retreat.
2. Here the laws of supply and demand work very much in your favor: Advertising rates are a lot cheaper so your company and its products get a lot more bang for the advertising buck.

Strategically, it is of course important for your advertising campaign to continue to focus on increasing unit sales during a recession. However, it is strategically even more important to broaden your advertising campaign in a way that focuses more on the longer-term goal of building your brand. In fact, recessions are a great time to build brand precisely for the two reasons just stated: The advertising market is far less crowded and ad rates are a lot cheap.

Dell Takes on the Big Boys

> When times are tougher, you've got to be more aggressive. Your growth has to come from market share captured from somebody else. You have to be a predator.
> —Britt Beemer, Chairman, America's Research Group

Dell was not always the household name it is today. In fact, back during the 1990–1991 recession, the computer company was just a young upstart, and Michael Dell was as anonymous to the general public as any other John Doe.

With one brilliant Master Cyclist stroke, Young Mr. Dell would change all of that with one of the boldest countercyclical advertising campaigns in marketing history. During the recession, as major players in the computer industry like IBM and the now dear departed Digital were slashing their advertising budgets by almost 20%, Michael Dell increased his company's advertising budget by more than 300%.

By seizing the recessionary day in this way, Michael Dell was able to both build company brand and market share and also set the stage for Dell Computer's brilliant ascent during the 1990s.[2]

Buy a Hyundai, Return It If You Get Canned

Fast forward to the crash of 2007 to 2009, and you observe another lower-ranked player in a big industry using a very well-targeted and very well-envisioned countercyclical advertising campaign to seize market share from the bigger boys in a time of turbulence. Taking a page right out of the Master Cyclist playbook, South Korea's Hyundai Motor Group first countercyclically cut its advertising expenditures from $550 million in $2006 to $443 million in 2007 during the late stages of economic expansion. However, with the onset of the recession, Hyundai increased its advertising to $651 million in 2008 just as most companies were cutting back on their marketing.

With these increased advertising dollars, and in a brilliant masterstroke, Hyundai's marketing department introduced the perfect advertising program for troubled times on the grandest of stages the American Super Bowl. Directly addressing the growing angst in America, Hyundai offered up an "Assurance Plus program" designed to lure into automobile showrooms customers who might otherwise be worried about their jobs. Here's what Hyundai promised:

> If you lose your income, we'll make your payments for 3 months while you get back on your feet, and if that's not enough time to work things out, you can return the car with no impact on your credit.
>
> We're all in this together, and we think it'll be a little easier to get through it with a good set of wheels.

Said Jesse Toprak, the director of analysis for the auto-research firm Edmunds.com, "Hyundai's program seems to have really dealt with a core issue of making consumers feel more secure about a purchase."[3] In fact, Hyundai's executive team came up with the program after "its own market research showed car shoppers weren't attracted by rebates and other more normal incentives. . . . People are simply too worried about making payments no matter how good the deal is."[4]

The results of this countercyclically marketing coup were dramatic. While the sales of market leaders, such as Ford, GM, Honda, and the world's largest automaker, Toyota, all dropped significantly in the month after the campaign was launched, Hyundai's sales jumped 14%—this in the middle of a recession. (As a coda to this example, and proving once again that imitation is the sincerest form of flattery, many of the major automakers would belatedly adopt guarantees very similar to Hyundai's.)

CHANGE YOUR PRODUCT MIX AND MARKETING MESSAGES!

> *The housing industry. . . is a good example of marketing management action in a recession: Faced with growing uncertainty and slower-growing disposable income, on the one hand, and the rising cost of private homes, on the other, many potential buyers left the housing market. To cope with the situation of radically declining demand, many builders adjusted their marketing mix by offering smaller, cheaper houses.*
>
> —Professor Avraham Shama,
> University of New Mexico

This observation speaks to the fact that countercyclically increasing your advertising during a recession doesn't mean that you should simply throw more money at the very same marketing program you had in place before the recession began. Instead, as the case of Hyundai has already helped signal, your organization must change both its advertising messages *and* its product mix to match the changing moods of the business cycle seasons. Such a tactical refocusing of the product mix and product messages recognizes that many consumers respond more to product value than style in recessionary times.

Campbell Soup and El Pollo Loco Mix It Up

A Master Cyclist company that clearly knows how to retool its product mix and sell value in a recession is the Campbell Soup Company. During the toughest times of the 2007 to 2009 crash, Campbell's executive team used an aggressive, countercyclical advertising campaign to remind its customers of the iconic product's value as a highly nutritious, low-cost meal. Comarketing its low-cost soups with Kraft cheese singles, Campbell's tagline was vintage Master Cyclist: "The wallet-friendly meal your family will love."

Clearly, Campbell's countercyclical strategy paid off. It was the only stock in the entire Standard & Poor's 500 index to show gains when the credit crisis first hit. Moreover, during 2008, its sales grew 8% and net earnings jumped 36%.

Said Campbell's president and CEO Doug Conant at a 2008 earnings call on the virtues of countercyclical advertising and changing the product mix: "Growth in sales of select soups was primarily driven by higher advertising and promotional activity. . . . All of our marketing mix modeling suggests that the opportunity to revitalize the category and to grow is connected with the consumer now through trade promotions."

In a similar fashion, there is also the example of El Pollo Loco—the national fast food restaurant leader in flame-broiled chicken. What is perhaps most interesting about this example is that it helps illustrate why it is not always necessary to forecast the business cycle accurately in order to flexibly implement Master Cyclist management principles.

In fact, the 2001 recession caught El Pollo Loco's executive team totally flat-footed. However, with the onset of the recession and as demand and revenues began to fall at its stores, the executive team nimbly shifted its product line by aggressively promoting a "Leg and Thighs" deal that featured a very aggressive price point. By temporarily shifting its product line focus toward the much cheaper dark-meat end, El Pollo Loco's top management team could pass savings along to its customers, highlight a purely price-driven promotion, and get credit with its customers for offering an abundance of food at a great value. The results were both increased transactions and, most interestingly given the tough times, a higher check for the average customer.[5]

Ruby Tuesday's Untimely Descent into Rebranding Hell

> *Elevating Ruby Tuesday above the crowd to a memorable, high-*
> *quality dining experience is critical to our growth and success.* . . .
> *We began by bringing our guests fresh, exciting new menu choices,*
> *then raised our standards of service, and are now creating an*
> *innovative new look and style for each and every restaurant. This*
> *revitalization will appeal to our loyal core guests while attracting a*
> *new generation of consumers.*
> —Sandy Beall, CEO and Chairman, Ruby Tuesday, 2007

At the other end of the spectrum, it is also useful to remind our-selves of the extreme adverse consequences when a company fails to sell value heading into a recession. Consider, then, the bizarre marketing campaign of the restaurant chain Ruby Tuesday.

Just months before the onset of recession in 2007, and exhibit-ing the worst type of forecasting myopia imaginable, Ruby Tuesday's executive team began a rebranding program designed to move its restaurant chain up the value and pricing scale in the casual dining market. This rebranding program aimed at selling style over value was suicidal—and also involved average price increases of about $3 per meal.

For this Reactive Cyclist lapse in marketing judgment, Ruby Tuesday shareholders paid dearly: While stock prices for the restau-rant industry fell about 30% in the middle of the recession in 2008, Ruby Tuesday's shareholders took a 75% hit.

SYNERGIES OF COUNTERCYCLICAL ADVERTISING

As a final Master Cyclist marketing point: While it's important to think strategically about advertising over the business cycle seasons, it is equally important to think *synergistically* and *tactically*. In fact, during a recession, countercyclical advertising may be wielded as a great tactical weapon to synergistically trim any unwanted inventory buildups in selected product lines. This tactic also underscores the importance of business cycle management communication across the different functional silos of the firm—in this case the market-ing department and operations management.

One company that used this tactical tool very well in the early stages of the 2007 to 2009 crash was the Kohl's department store chain. Among retailers, Kohl's was one of the first retailers to see recessionary troubles on the horizon. As soon as its inventory began to build up, the company boosted its advertising to trim these inventories—even as competitors began to cut back.

At the same time, Kohl's quickly shifted its advertising messages towards the value spectrum. Said Kohl's CEO Kevin Mansell on its Master Cyclist strategic shift: "We're very focused on making sure that we can show [customers] that their dollar is going further."[6]

Action Item

Review your organization's advertising and marketing strategy over the course of the business cycle. Does it countercyclically advertise during recessions or have a tendency to cut advertising in tough times? Can your organization nimbly change its product mix and advertising messages to sell value in tough times and style in good times?

CHAPTER

19

Why Companies Often Price Their Products and Manage Credit Exactly Wrong

Ford and Vauxhall sparked criticism tonight by increasing the price of their cars by up to £1,000 in the wake of falling sales, the recession and a massive taxpayer bail-out. The inflation-busting rises by Britain's two biggest car companies come at a time when customers expect showroom prices to be falling. The move was condemned as "idiotic" and "suicidal" by critics.

—Daily Mail Online

While most business cycle management strategies are implemented countercyclically, the rule for properly pricing the business cycle is to do so *procyclically*. As a general rule, you should raise your prices when the economy is expanding to boost revenues. Even more critical to protecting your bottom line—and market share!—you should cut prices when the economy is entering a recession.

Unfortunately, as the above excerpt from the United Kingdom's second largest-selling newspaper demonstrates, far too many executive teams raise their prices during recessions for one simple reason:

desperation. It is a desperation that comes about from rapidly shrinking profit margins and a plummeting stock price.

DON'T RAISE PRICES OUT OF DESPERATION!

The inevitable knee-jerk reaction to such desperation is to raise prices to offset falling revenues. The equally inevitable result is that revenues fall even faster, and your company's balance sheet falls into a dangerous downward spiral. A classic case in point involves the pricing "strategy"—and the term is used very loosely here—of Goodyear Tires, the number-one tire maker in North America and Latin America.[1]

Goodyear Drives a Pricing Spike into Its Profits

In the year and a half leading up to the March 2001 recession, Goodyear's executive team faced an increasingly ugly triangle of business cycle–related problems. For starters, during the 1990s, the company had assumed a very heavy debt load, and this was causing cash flow and liquidity problems as the economy began to soften. On top of this, the euro began to weaken significantly in 2000. This falling euro cut deeply into the profits of Goodyear, Europe's second-largest tire maker, further exacerbating its cash flow problems.

Adding further bottom-line injury, oil prices began to spike in the latter half of 2000 as the longest-running economic expansion in global history was coming to a climax. This oil price spike put further cost pressures on Goodyear because almost 70% of the raw materials used to manufacture tires are derived from crude oil.

At this point, while the economy was in the last gasps of its expansion, Goodyear raised its prices; at least at this point, that was all well and good. Revenues rose along with Goodyear profits. With the onset of the March 2001 recession, however, market conditions began to change dramatically. Not only did demand for Goodyear tires in the replacement market begin to fall off, but new vehicle sales dropped sharply as well—and the demand for Goodyear tires from auto manufacturers along with it.

Caught in a cash flow squeeze and seemingly oblivious to the deteriorating market conditions, Goodyear reacted like the most business cycle–insensitive Reactive Cyclist imaginable. The company didn't just raise its prices again; it raised its prices three more times!

Not only did this price gouging not raise company revenues. It helped the company lose more than $200 million that year while the stock price of Goodyear fell from a high of $31 per share in 2000 to less than $7 by 2002.

The irony of all of this is that in its 2000 annual report, Goodyear's executive team had declared: "We will be aggressive in increasing prices where market conditions allow." Unfortunately, the very next year, that executive team remembered only the part about being "aggressive" and completely forgot about the need to monitor those pesky "market conditions."

Sony Loses the Playstation 3 versus Xbox 360 Pricing Wars to Microsoft

December '08 was the biggest month for Xbox 360 in history. In the all-important holiday quarter, Xbox 360 outsold PS3 by more than 2:1. . . . Not only did the Xbox 360 see its weekly sales run rate increase 38 percent compared to November, it also continued to outperform the PS3 [PlayStation 3] by two-to-one for the third month in a row.

—Michael McWhertor, *Kotaku, the Gamer's Guide*

Let's fast forward now to the crash of 2007 to 2009 and review the sharply contrasting pricing strategies of Microsoft versus Sony for their gaming consoles during the recession-plagued holiday season in 2008. This Xbox 360 versus PlayStation 3 pricing war illustrates more broadly both the benefits and costs of executing—or failing to execute—timely price cuts during recessionary times.

Microsoft's executive team saw early on that the 2008 holiday season was shaping up to be one of the worst on record. It responded with a series of steep price cuts for its Xbox 360 as early as July. In contrast, as late in the holiday season as October 2008, Sony continued to resist any such price cuts, announcing "We aren't making any price moves [for the PlayStation 3] this holiday."[2]

Microsoft's price cuts helped propel the Xbox 360 to its biggest holiday sales ever—"despite a decline in overall consumer spending." Microsoft's procyclical pricing strategy also helped the Xbox 360 "outperform PS3 by two-to-one" for the last three months of the year.

Toyota Seizes Defeat from the Jaws of Victory

While Sony's pricing miscue was hardly surprising—it has a reputation as an inflexible behemoth—a similar kind of misstep by Toyota took the automobile world by complete surprise. Cruising confidently down the road toward the crash of 2007 to 2009, Toyota had everything going for it. It had a pile of cash and a fleet of popular, fuel-efficient vehicles; and it was already overtaking GM as the world's largest auto manufacturer.

Then, in May of 2008, seemingly oblivious to the economy collapsing around it, the overconfident company got cocky. It not only raised the prices on a wide variety of Toyota and Lexus vehicles; it also further jacked up the premium on its best-selling Prius hybrid. To the company's everlasting surprise, by November of that year, cars began to pile up on the docks in Long Beach, California, where many Japanese vehicles arrive from Japan to be transported across the United States.

Faced with this backlog, the company that had long used fast inventory turns to boost its bottom line was forced to rent barges, lots, and warehouses to store unsold inventory for months. On top of this, the company had to temporarily shut down some plants in both the United States and Japan and lay off many of its temps and contract workers. Meanwhile, as we saw in Chapter 18, the nimble Master Cyclist Hyundai of Korea ran market share–grabbing circles around its clueless Japanese rival.

WHY ELASTICITY OF DEMAND IS CRITICAL TO PRICING STRATEGY

> *Knowing the elasticity of demand for your products. . . is a key to determining pricing strategy.*
> —James Stotter, Founder, Busimetrics

The kind of desperate pricing behavior evinced by Goodyear and the ostrichlike behavior demonstrated by Sony and Toyota can happen only through a fundamental lack of economic literacy and a corresponding failure to understand one of the most important concepts in economics: price elasticity of demand.

Price elasticity of demand measures the percentage drop in the demand for a product for any given percentage change in price.

For example, if a 10% increase in price leads to a corresponding 10% decrease in price, demand is said to be unit elastic, and the elasticity of demand equals –1.0. In such a case, a price hike or price decrease will have no impact on total revenues as the percentage change in price is exactly offset by the percentage change in quantity demanded.

In contrast, if a large price hike leads to an even larger percentage drop in consumer demand for a product, demand is said to be highly elastic in much the same way that a rubber band stretches significantly when you pull it. In such a case, any attempt to raise prices will lead to a fall in total revenues and likely a corresponding reduction in profits. This is because the revenue benefits of any price hike will be more than offset by the revenue losses due to fewer units sold.

Now, here's a dirty little secret that you almost certainly were not taught in any undergraduate economics course—or even in your MBA studies if you went to business school. Demand elasticities are decidedly not static or immutable. Instead, they change significantly over the business cycle seasons.

In particular, demand elasticities tend to become *less* elastic during expansions. Intuitively, when consumers are flush with cash and life is good, they are simply much less price sensitive. That's precisely why you should procyclically raise prices during expansions.

On the other side of the business cycle ledger—and this is where the real danger lies—demand elasticities tend to become significantly *more* elastic during recessions. Again intuitively, unemployed consumers and consumers concerned about their job prospects save more and spend less and become much more price sensitive.

What this means for strategically pricing the business cycle is this: If you have priced your product correctly during an expansion and a recession ensues, you must reprice your product as soon as possible to continue to maximize your total revenues and profits. You must do so to counteract the negative effects on your total revenues of any increase in the price elasticity of demand for your product as the recession takes hold.

Apple's Plastic, Incredibly Price-Elastic iPhone

One company that has exhibited a very high level of sophistication in understanding the importance of the elasticity of demand in pricing strategy is Apple. To see what I mean, consider the economic logic behind how Apple moved its iPhone pricing from $599 to $399 and finally to $199.

At the initial release of the iPhone, Apple's executive team clearly understood that price would be highly *inelastic* and therefore relatively price insensitive. This is because at this time, customer interest was at its peak, economic times were good, and there was a huge pent-up demand for Apple's latest innovation. Ergo, the initial whopping price of $599.

However, as the iPhone went into mass production and use and the economy softened, the executive team also understood that the elasticity of demand for the iPhone would become more and more elastic. In order to maximize sales and revenues, Apple therefore would have to find progressively lower price points. That's why Apple moved the iPhone price first to $399 and then to $199.

At the same time that it was cutting the iPhone's price, Apple also arranged with its partner, AT&T, to pick up a larger portion of the monthly services fee to further reduce the effective price. As Apple's chief financial officer, Peter Oppenheimer, noted in a January 2009 conference call, "There is clearly price elasticity." Said Oppenheimer of the iPhone's final price point:

> We feel the $199 price is a compelling value and see nothing in the market that even comes close. We feel we are years ahead of the competition. . . . We are very happy with elasticity we have seen, and think the trade-off between volume and price was a good one. . . . The goal was not leaving an umbrella so big as to leave an opportunity for our competitors.

In the language of the Master Cyclist, Apple clearly recognized that "the trade-off between volume and price was a good one," meaning that at this point, Apple's profits would be maximized. As an added strategic benefit, this price point would also be low enough to ward off any iPhone "competitors" and thus serve as what economists call a barrier to entry into the market.

Apple Names the Right Price for that iTune

The deft repricing of its iPhone was hardly the only demonstration of Apple's Master Cyclist agility during this difficult economic period. As an outgrowth of its wildly successful iPod campaign, Apple has casually picked up a side gig as the world's largest music distributor. In fact, while CD sales have declined steadily in recent years, Apple's music sales and its market share have climbed just as steadily.

In late 2007, in a rapid Master Cyclist response to both a changing music market and a deteriorating economy, Apple dropped the price of its Digital Rights Management music from $1.29 per song to just 99 cents per tune. (Apple's Digital Rights Management allowed it to prevent the free transfer of any song beyond the original buyer).

This was just a start, however. In January of 2009, citing further pressure on consumers' pocketbooks and arguing that their product had no marginal cost of production, Apple further slashed the price of many of its songs to just 69 cents. Even more importantly, Apple abandoned its Digital Rights Management system altogether and now offers all of the 10 million songs in its library without copy protection—even as it allows iPhone users to download songs through their 3G wireless networks.

These moves are likely to put the last nail in the coffin of traditional music resellers. At the same time, these aggressive Master Cyclist tactics are likely to keep Apple's trailing online competitors at bay.

MANAGING CREDIT OVER THE BUSINESS CYCLE

Closely related to the problem of strategically pricing the cycle is when to loosen or tighten credit and when to collect accounts receivable more aggressively. While these credit management tasks may not be among the sexiest in your organization, performing them well—or poorly—is often the difference between a profitable and an unprofitable quarter during a recession.

The typical Reactive Cyclist mistake is to continue to loosen the credit reins well into the late stages of an economic expansion. The equally typical result is a mountain of uncollectible accounts receivable once the recession hits and large write-downs that take big bites from your bottom line. One company that had to write down literally *billions* of dollars in uncollectible receivables for committing this Reactive Cyclist sin is the telecom network gear provider Lucent.[3]

Lucent Buries Itself under a Mound of Uncollectible Accounts Receivable

During the heyday of the technology bubble in the late 1990s, and well before it merged with the European telecom giant Alcatel,

Lucent was at the top of the heap of tech darlings in the telecom space. With an aristocratic pedigree—it was spun off from AT&T in 1996—the company was blessed with one of the most powerful engines of innovation the world has ever seen, the vaunted Bell Laboratories. Indeed, it was Bell Labs that gave us incredible innovations ranging from the transistor and lasers to cell phone technology, communications satellites, and even the touchtone phone.

Regrettably, Lucent's credit management brilliance proved no match for its scientific genius. In fact, right into the very teeth of the 2001 recession, and right as Lucent continued to myopically fight a brutal market share war with arch competitor Nortel, Lucent continued to offer huge credit financing packages to high-risk start-up companies. In effect, Lucent's credit managers were saying "Here, take whatever gear you want now and just pay us later"—oblivious to the mounting risk of default in a rapidly deteriorating economy.

Of course, when many of these dot-com companies went belly up, Lucent was unable to collect a huge chuck of this growing mountain of IOUs. In the bitter recessionary end, Lucent would have to write down an astonishing sum—more than $4 *billion* in uncollectible accounts receivable.

Discover Folds Its Cards in Florida and California

Our results and financial position reflect our conservative
orientation toward growth, credit risk and capital management as
we position Discover to weather the economic downturn.
> —David Nelms, CEO, Discover Financial Services, 2008
> Fourth-Quarter Earnings Report

At the other end of the credit management spectrum, Master Cyclist organizations never allow their accounts receivable to get out of hand. At the first sign of any possible recession, these organizations begin to pull in their accounts receivable more aggressively even as they begin to tighten credit. In this way, the Master Cyclist credit manager preempts any problem of uncollectible receivables.

Discover Financial Services offers an excellent variation on this theme. Its executive team astutely began to tighten credit in anticipation of the crash of 2007 to 2009.

Sensing the recessionary and credit crisis minefields ahead as early as the peak of the housing and mortgage drunkenness, the team stopped aggressively adding new cardholders in the two markets most vulnerable to the collapse of the housing bubble: Florida and California. David Nelms, Discover's chief executive, put it simply: "Managing our business conservatively has helped (us) weather a tough economic environment."[4] The company also raised the top rate it charges to risky new card customers and raised late fees for most of its customers. Given these credit management strategies, it is hardly surprising that Discover has one of the lowest delinquency rates in the industry.

As a final comment on the credit management front, it isn't just uncollectible accounts receivable that the Master Cyclist credit manager worries about, however. Strategically, it is almost as important to *loosen* credit quickly during a recession when a new economic expansion is on the horizon. In this way, credit management serves a dual function as a useful marketing tool. Easier credit during a recession helps retain existing customers and attract new ones.

Action Item

Carefully review your organization's pricing and credit management strategies over the last two recessions with an eye toward Master Cyclist pricing and credit rules. Determine whether your organization is prone to raising prices when times are tough and thereby shooting itself in the foot. Discuss with your marketing department whether the concept of the price elasticity of demand is ever incorporated into the pricing calculus. Check how much it has cost your organization to write down its uncollectible accounts receivable during the last two economic downturns.

20

How To Not Get Run Over by the Capital Expenditures Bandwagon

I see an unparalleled opportunity to gain market share and expand business. The downturn has left some of our very heavily leveraged competitors weak and unable to invest in their businesses. By investing, we're a leg up and in better position to get new business or take away existing business from somebody else.
— King Harris, CEO, Pittway Corporation

These words of wisdom accurately and astutely capture the rewards of properly timing your organization's capital expenditures over the ups and downs of the business cycle as well as the substantial risks involved in failing to do so.[1] When it comes to capital expenditures, your Master Cyclist management mantra should be:

- Cut capital expenditures in anticipation of a recession to build up your cash position and avoid overcapacity.
- Increase your capital expenditures during recessions so as to be first to market with products that reflect the latest innovations and styles.

Far too many organizations engage in just the opposite kind of investment behavior. These Reactive Cyclists embark on wild capital spending sprees in the late stages of an economic expansion, sprees that leave them in a heavily leveraged position with an overhang of overcapacity. Of course, once the recession hits, these Reactive Cyclists dramatically cut their capital expenditures and wind up losing out to their more innovative Master Cyclist rivals once the economy recovers.

CUT YOUR CAPITAL EXPENDITURES BEFORE A RECESSION

The failure to cut capital expenditures in anticipation of a recession happens to organizations for any one of a number of reasons. The most obvious is that an organization may have failed to sufficiently develop and deploy sufficient forecasting capabilities. Without any capability to look clearly into the future, the organization winds up being caught totally by surprise at the onset of a recession.

An equally common and often collateral problem is that an organization may fall prey to the so-called bandwagon effect. The bandwagon effect refers to the well-known tendency of firms in cyclical industries to overbuild their capacity during the expansionary phase of the business cycle. The central problem is that the executive teams of these organizations tend to watch their rivals far too closely when they should be keeping at least one eye out for any signs of a looming recessionary turning point.

Here's the typical bandwagon effect scenario: As the economy continues to boom in the late stages of an economic expansion, product demand grows at an ever faster rate. Believing that such growth will last forever, the Reactive Cyclist executive team launches ever more ambitious capital expansion programs to meet its projections of future demand. However, absent an adequate forecasting capability, this myopic and industry-centric executive team bases its demand projections not on broader economic conditions but rather simply on industry trends.

In undertaking these capital expenditures at this critical phase of the business cycle, this Reactive Cyclist organization inevitably suffers a double whammy—even before its real troubles begin. The first whammy is that the organization incurs higher construction costs. This is because the costs of real bricks and mortar are at their highest in the overheated economy.

The second whammy is that the financing costs of these capital expenditures are likely to be at their highest as well. This is because, in the late stage of an economic expansion, inflationary pressures are building, and interest rates are likely to be rising rapidly.

Here is the truly fatal error that so many Reactive Cyclist organizations make when they find themselves propelled along on the capital expansion bandwagon: These organizations choose to finance their capital expenditure programs using heavy debt financing.

The obvious problem with taking on massive amounts of new debt just before a recession is that this additional debt burden leaves an organization in a very heavily leveraged position once the economy turns down. While the organization's revenues are plummeting, its debt obligations remain a burdensome constant.

It is precisely in such times that many organizations become the heavily leveraged and weak competitors mentioned in the quotation leading off this chapter. They simply don't have the cash flow to cover their debts and often are forced into extreme measures— from seeking bankruptcy protection to selling off prime chunks of the organization. One of the best examples of this destructive behavior from the crash of 2007 to 2009 crash is offered up by the Chesapeake Corporation.

Chesapeake Spends Itself Into Bankruptcy

Richmond-based Chesapeake Corp. has filed for Chapter 11 bankruptcy protection and plans to sell itself to a group of investors for about $485 million. . . . The company, founded in Virginia in 1918, has struggled with a heavy debt load and difficulty raising capital in the tight credit markets.

—Richmond Times-Dispatch

Rather than trim capital expenditures in anticipation of the recession to preserve cash flow, Chesapeake's executive team did just the opposite. The team almost doubled capital expenditures in its plastics packaging division just as the recession approached.[2] Moreover, these expenditures were financed largely with expensive debt that created a heavy cash flow burden for the company once the recession hit.

After all but destroying his company with his Reactive Cyclist miscue, Chesapeake's chastened president and chief executive officer (CEO), Andrew J. Kohut, would have to make this ultimate embarrassing statement: "to maintain the liquidity we need to operate our businesses in an extremely difficult economic environment . . . a court-supervised sale of our business operations is in the best interest of the company and its stakeholders."

In contrast to this typical bandwagon effect scenario, the Master Cyclist organization begins cutting capital expenditures in anticipation of a recession. In this way, the Master Cyclist organization begins building its recessionary cash war chest for when times get tough.

Being in a strong cash position as a recession hits is the best of all possible worlds. Not only does it allow an organization to engage in capital expenditures that will position it best for the recovery. It also provides the purchasing power for aggressively engaging in the kind of buy-low acquisition strategies we discuss at length in Chapter 21.

The contrasting cases of Johnson & Johnson (J&J) and the merchant electricity generator Calpine graphically illustrate both the rewards and risks of strategic capital expenditures management on the upward slope of the business cycle.

J&J Circles Its Capital Expenditures Bandwagon

We saw this recession coming three years ago. It was obvious the booming economic cycle couldn't continue. We tightened our belts. We focused on cash flow.
— Ralph Larsen, CEO, Johnson & Johnson

This observation perfectly epitomizes the mind-set of the Master Cyclist executive even as it highlights the company's flawless execution of countercyclically cutting capital expenditures in anticipation of a recession. At the very height of the economic boom in 2000, J&J's executive team took the highly unusual step of cutting its capital expenditures by more than $100 million—a bold move that initially had both shareholders and financial analysts scratching their heads. After all, this was J&J's first capital expenditures cut in seven years; and to the layperson, times still seemed very good.

Such second-guessing notwithstanding, J&J's pitch-perfect contrarian move allowed the company to build up its cash reserves and thereby be in a strong cash position once the 2001 recession hit.

The performance results were outstanding: "As the company significantly built up its cash reserves, it saw double-digit growth in revenues and earnings."[3]

Calpine Drives Its Expansion Bandwagon Over a Cliff

> *Soaring electricity prices and sizzling investor interest fueled a boom period for the company, but it descended into bankruptcy protection in 2005 under the weight of a debt-laden expansion that backfired.*
> —*Los Angeles Times*

While Johnson & Johnson was busy cutting its capital expenditures in anticipation of the 2001 recession, the San Jose, California–based merchant electricity generator Calpine was getting ready to become a synonym for hubris. In February 2001, just one month before the recession would begin—and almost a year *after* the yield curve had inverted to warn of recession—Calpine's CEO, Peter Cartwright, announced one of the most aggressive capital expansion programs in modern electric utility industry history.

Calpine's astonishing goal was to increase its generating base of 10,000 megawatts sevenfold within four years. This expansion "would be the equivalent of building more than *fifty* new nuclear power plants and would make Calpine the largest power producer in the country."[4] This procyclical capital expenditure program on the very eve of a recession would turn out, however, to be an absolute Reactive Cyclist train wreck.

As the recession took hold, Calpine's revenue plunged; and its cash flow wasn't nearly enough to service its more than $20 billion of debt. For the next several years, Calpine would repeatedly flirt with bankruptcy until the company finally succumbed to Chapter 11 in December 2005. Thanks to the hubris of the company's CEO, Calpine shareholders saw the value of their shares go from $60 to a whopping 16 cents.

RAMP UP CAPITAL EXPENDITURES DURING A RECESSION

As important as it is to cut your capital expenditures in anticipation of a recession and build your cash position, it is even more important to countercyclically *increase* capital expenditures once a recession hits. By doing so, your organization will be first to market with products that reflect the latest innovations and styles. Moreover, this first-to-market effect is all the more amplified in higher-technology industries with shorter product cycles.

It's not just that building new capacity in a recession allows you to offer the most advanced products. Countercyclical capital expenditure programs have other advantages as well.

For one thing, building a state-of-the-art production facility will allow your organization to produce its products at the lowest possible cost. This translates into pricing power over your competitors.

In addition, the costs of capital, construction labor, equipment, and raw materials all tend to be lower during a recession. That's an additional cost advantage.

In fact, the reigning master of all Master Cyclists practicing this countercyclical investment strategy is Intel Corporation—the largest manufacturer of semiconductors in the world.

Intel's Reigning Masters of the Recessionary Universe

New technology is what pulls companies in technology out of recessions. The opportunity cost of not having that capacity when demand recovers is astronomical. . . . Our perspective is: we make these investments now, and it will take us 18–24 months to bring them online in totality, and we'll be able to run those for another two years after that. We are making very long lead time investments. This new technology will lower our cost, and give us a more competitive product.
    —Paul Otellini, President and CEO, Intel Corporation

As this quotation from Paul Otellini in February 2009[5] affirms, the strategic application of countercyclical investment is embedded deep in Intel's organizational culture. Indeed, as Intel's cofounder Gordon Moore observed long ago: "Recessions always end and innovation allows some companies to emerge from them stronger than before."

A classic example of Intel's well-timed capital expenditures strategy is offered up by its big wafer–small technology gambit during the 2001 recession. While many of its competitors were retrenching during the downturn, Intel sharply accelerated its capital spending. The bulk of this investment was directed into building additional manufacturing capacity using two new cost-saving innovations—"jumbo" wafer production and a smaller 0.13-micron technology. Through these innovations, Intel was able to manufacture higher-performance chips that were smaller and faster, cost less to manufacture, and even cost less to operate because they use less power.

When the 2002–2003 recovery came, Intel nimbly and quickly launched new products months ahead of schedule, such as its Centrino mobile processor technology and Mobile Pentium IV-M processor. After these new products hit the market, Intel reported its highest rate of growth since 1996 and saw its net income rise by 81%.[6]

Intel's executive team has likewise sought to take advantage of the many opportunities offered by the crash of 2007 to 2009. In the darkest days of that crash, Intel invested more than $7 billion on four new manufacturing facilities.[7] These investments will allow Intel to maintain its lead in PC microprocessor manufacturing technologies over its rival Advanced Micro Devices.

These new investments will also help the company move into other markets where smaller, more efficient chips are required, such as in embedded devices and cell phones. Inevitably, during a recession, cash-strapped competitors fall months behind Intel in terms of cutting-edge technologies and are unable to compete effectively on cost once a recovery ensues. Using its Master Cyclist weapons, Intel is thus able to maintain gross margins significantly higher than industry averages.

As a final comment, it is worth pointing out that the Intel executive team holds the highest degree of economic literacy; and this literacy permeates Intel's broader organizational culture. In particular, Paul Otellini's observation about the "opportunity cost of not having that [new] capacity when demand recovers is astronomical" reflects a very sophisticated understanding of a key economic concept. In this case, the "opportunity cost" that Otellini refers to speaks directly to the enormous opportunities lost when a company like Intel is not ready to meet market demand with new products in a recovering economy.

DuPont Modernizes while Rivals Batten Down the Recessionary Hatches

Of course, increasing your capital expenditures during a recession doesn't necessarily always mean adding new capacity. A recession also offers an excellent time to replace or modernize existing facilities because the opportunity costs of lost capacity utilization are relatively low.

Another classic case in point involves the DuPont chemical company. As 1999 ended with record profits for DuPont, its forecasting team began to issue warnings about the recessionary effects that soaring raw materials costs, rising interest rates, higher oil prices, and weaker housing starts were likely to have on what by then was one of the longest economic expansions in U.S. history.

In response to these forecasting concerns, DuPont's executive team cut its capital expenditures in 2001 by fully $400 million—a 20% reduction. As the recession deepened, DuPont quickly accelerated the pace of its modernization programs as well as the shutdown of its aging facilities. Its overarching broader goal was to change the company's product mix in response to changing global economic conditions.[8]

Action Item

Review your organization's patterns of capital expenditures going out of the last two recessions. Determine whether your organization is more of a Reactive Cyclist subject to the bandwagon effect and the dangers of being heavily leveraged in a recession or a Master Cyclist organization that countercyclically times its capital expenditures for strategic advantage.

21

Why You Should Buy Low and Sell High over the Stock Market Cycle

How firms pursue strategies that take advantage of time-specific opportunities, such as whether to enter an industry during an upturn or downturn, is one of the great unexplored themes of strategic organization.
       —Professor John Matthews, Macquarie University

This observation from a prominent Australian strategy professor aptly highlights the Achilles' heel of modern corporate strategy: its failure to appropriately consider *timing* in the execution of many strategic decisions over the course of the business cycle. Nowhere is this failure more evident than in the area of strategic acquisitions and divestitures.

From a theoretical perspective, the field of corporate strategy teaches that there are many reasons why one organization may want to acquire another. One reason is to get rid of a rival and thereby gain more pricing power in that industry. A second may be to take control of a key element of your supply chain. A third reason may be that an acquisition provides important synergies—for example, a credit-scoring software company such as Fair Isaac might benefit from a new predictive technology developed by a another software company that may not be a direct competitor. Still a fourth reason may be that an acquisition offers the benefits of either a broad industry diversification or a global diversification—as we see in the cases of Berkshire Hathaway and Marubeni.

Regardless of the rationale for any acquisition, it is essential that any executive team obey this all-important maxim:

> Any acquisition must be accretive to earnings.

In a Master Cyclist and an Always a Winner context, this maxim means that no matter how attractive an acquisition may seem from a strategic perspective, if its purchase price is too high, that acquisition will *never* be accretive to earnings. To put this crucial point another way:

> Any overpriced acquisition—no matter how many benefits it may convey—will never overcome its high costs and add to the company's bottom line.

Ultimately, then, the primary determinant of whether acquisition is accretive to earnings will be its purchase price. For a publicly traded company, its purchase price, of course, relates directly to its stock price. Given that this is true, we must firmly dispense with one of the great hoaxes of modern corporate finance, namely, that the stock market is some kind of meandering, trendless random walk.

WHY THE RANDOM WALK IS RUBBISH

While it is true that on any given day, and perhaps in any given week, it is difficult to predict the direction of the stock market, it is equally true that, over time, the stock market moves through long periods of clearly identifiable trends. As a rule, bull markets tend to trend up for relatively longer periods of time during economic expansions.

Bear markets tend to trend down much more sharply and for shorter periods of time in anticipation of, and during, recessions.

To see these undeniably *non*random patterns, take a look at Exhibit 21.1.

You can clearly see in the exhibit that between 1993 and 2008, the stock market, as measured by movements in the Standard & Poor's 500 Index, enjoyed two relatively long bullish up-trends—one from January 1995 to August 2000 and another from September 2002 until October 2007. The exhibit likewise clearly illustrates two steeper and shorter bearish downtrends that began after each of the two bull markets hit their market tops.

Clearly, there is nothing random or trendless about these patterns. Equally clearly, very large price differentials exist between these bull market tops and bear market bottoms—differentials that reflect price swings of up to 30% to 40%. These large price differentials clearly imply the need to incorporate a buy low, sell high strategic mind-set into your acquisition and divestiture plans—timing *is* everything, certainly when it comes to this strategic business cycle management dimension.

Exhibit 21.1   Buying Low and Selling High over the Stock Market's Bullish and Bearish Trends

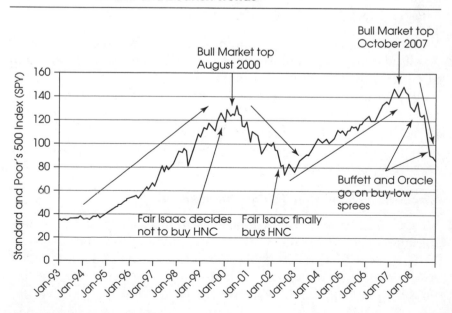

As for why the stock market cycle moves in a nonrandom pattern, we already know the answer. As Chapter 14 explained, the stock market is a leading indicator of the business cycle and stock prices reflect nothing more than a future stream of earnings.

When investors expect a robust economic expansion, they bid prices up on expectations of higher earnings. As long as these expectations hold, the stock market will trend upward.

Conversely, when investors anticipate a recession, they lower their earnings expectations, and they begin to sell their shares. As long as this expectation holds, the stock market will trend downward. Two obvious conclusions can be drawn from these observations.

1. The best time for your organization to make any acquisition it views as strategic is during the bearish phase of the stock market cycle. By buying low during this stock market phase, your organization has the best chance to make any purchase accretive to earnings.
2. By similar logic, the best time for your organization to divest any of its assets or units—or perhaps even sell the whole company off to a suitor—is during the bullish phase of the stock market and the collateral-happy expansionary economic times.

WHY GOOD COMPANIES MAKE BADLY TIMED ACQUISITIONS

While the age-old recommendation to buy low and sell high in your acquisitions and divestiture strategy would seem to make eminent good sense, far too many organizations refuse to follow this Master Cyclist advice. That sad fact of Reactive Cyclist life is reflected in this fact: For any given acquisition or divestiture, there must always be both a buyer and a seller. By definition, one party to that transaction must always be getting its timing wrong, at least near stock market tops and bottoms.

Wachovia's "Transformative" Self-Immolation

One of the most darkly comic examples of a Reactive Cyclist buying high at the peak of a stock market bubble is offered up by the banking and financial services company Wachovia. In May 2006, in the midst of a subprime lending frenzy and just as the housing bubble had begun to burst, Wachovia purchased the subprime mortgage lender Golden West Financial to further beef up its loan servicing and mortgage operations. To consummate the deal, Wachovia's executive team had to pony up a massively inflated price of $25 billion. This was nearly three times the firm's book value, five times its annual revenue, and almost $3 billion in excess of its peak market capitalization. The darkly comic part of this example may be found in how Wachovia's chief executive, Ken Thompson, described the acquisition. Prophetically—but in a way in which Thompson never dreamed—Thompson grandly declared: "This is a *transformative* deal for us."

Prior to the deal, Wachovia was America's fourth largest bank in market value. However, on the day the deal was announced, Wachovia's market capitalization dropped by $1 billion. Months later, as the first signs of the subprime mortgage crisis began to surface, Wachovia's investment would, for all practical purposes, vaporize.

In its final "transformation" in October 2008, Wachovia, facing the bankruptcy gallows, would be rescued by Wells Fargo for a song—with an all-stock deal allowing Wells Fargo to dramatically increase its customer base without forking over gobs of cash. *Transformative* indeed!

So why do so many Reactive Cyclists buy high and sell low? As with so many foibles of the Reactive Cyclist, this mistake can be traced back to factors such as a lack of any business cycle orientation within the organization, a corresponding failure to deploy adequate forecasting resources, and the cultural belief that good times never end. Any organization that has this kind of mind-set will focus on what sound strategic reasons there might be for an acquisition but likely ignore the crucial dynamic component of timing and the importance of purchase price in the accretive-to-earnings calculus.

Fair Isaac and MatlinPatterson Patiently Wait, Then Pounce!

One organization that never makes these kinds of mistakes is Fair Isaac. This Minneapolis-based Master Cyclist helps clients in 80 countries around the world manage credit risk, cut fraud losses, and meet their regulatory requirements.

In this role, Fair Isaac serves as the world's leading provider of decision management software as well as the leading supplier of so-called FICO scores, which are used to calculate the risk that a borrower will default on a loan or mortgage. In fact, Fair Isaac has already sold over one billion FICO scores to various credit bureaus and financial institutions.

Of course, you might expect a company that specializes in decision management software to be keenly attuned to issues such as the need to time decisions around the business cycle. Fair Isaac demonstrated this sensitivity in one of the more legendary well-timed acquisitions in modern corporate history.

Fair Isaac's acquisition target was a company called HNC Software. HNC was a 1986 spin-off from the U.S. Department of Defense; and Fair Isaac was well aware that HNC owned a patented form of predictive technology that could be applied to forecast human behavior across a broad range of activities and applications. As such, this predictive technology promised to provide Fair Isaac with powerful synergies: The deal would wed Fair Isaac's vaunted credit scoring software with HNC's powerful fraud detection algorithms.

When Fair Isaac first considered acquiring HNC Software in 1999, its executive team considered the price to be far too rich. Remember: As Exhibit 21.1 shows, this was a time when the stock market was in the very late stages of its irrationally exuberant bull market run.

For the next three years, Fair Isaac closely monitored the stock price of HNC Software. During this time, as that stock price continued to fall with the broader bear market, Fair Isaac resisted the urge to pull the trigger on the acquisition.

Finally, in April 2002, and very near to the stock market bottom, Fair Isaac swooped in and grabbed HNC Software at a very steep discount to its 1999 price. Within a year after buying HNC, Fair Isaac's revenue jumped 60% while its income more than quadrupled. In this way, this acquisition was accretive to earnings in spades.[1]

The private equity firm MatlinPatterson Global Advisers, a specialist in acquiring positions in distressed firms, illustrated a very similar kind of patience during the crash of 2007 to 2009. As the housing bubble completely deflated in 2007, MatlinPatterson began to look to acquire a bargain homebuilder.

After months of deliberations—and further deterioration in the stock prices of the homebuilder crowd—MatlinPatterson finally made its move in the middle of 2008. For $530 million, it grabbed a two-thirds stake in America's eleventh largest homebuilder, Standard Pacific, which had seen its stock plunge from $22 to $3.50. As Standard Pacific's chief executive officer (CEO) and turnaround specialist Ken Campbell observed after the cash infusion took his company off life support, MatlinPatterson "likes to invest in cyclical business at the bottom of the cycle."[2]

Micron and Oracle Sweep the Bottom

While the case of Fair Isaac illustrates how synergies drive some acquisitions, the examples of Micron and Oracle illustrate several additional compelling reasons for strategic acquisitions—and the power of timing such acquisitions with the business and stock market cycles.

Micron is one of the world's leading providers of advanced semiconductor solutions. The company makes a variety of computer chips used in applications ranging from computers and cell phones, to digital cameras and gaming systems.

Micron is also one of the world's leading Master Cyclist buy-low strategists. In fact, one of the specialties for which it has become famous is buying chip factories from competitors at the bottom of the semiconductor cycle to eliminate rivals and increase market share while cutting costs and expanding production in anticipation of the next cyclical upturn.

Consider Micron's 1998 acquisitions coup. In a sharply deteriorating chip market, Micron scooped up four internationally dispersed chip fabrication facilities from a then-weakened Texas Instruments. Strategically, these acquisitions allowed Micron to diversify its chip production geographically even as the acquisition eliminated significant capacity of a key rival and helped Micron firm up prices.

Micron struck again in April 2002 when it took advantage of a recession-battered Toshiba to buy a chip factory valued at about $2 billion for only $300 million. This purchase likewise eliminated a key rival in the market and helped allow pricing to return to profitability. Said Micron's CEO of the acquisition at the time: "This transaction clearly demonstrates Micron's commitment to further strengthen its memory business in the face of a significant industry downturn."[3]

During the crash of 2007 to 2009, the software giant Oracle executed an even grander buy-low strategy than Micron that will perfectly position the company once recovery comes. The *Wall Street Journal* has described Oracle's Master Cyclist move perhaps the best:

> While most American corporations pinch pennies, Oracle Corp. is quietly going on a shopping spree. The software giant completed 10 acquisitions in the past year, ranging from a maker of insurance-policy-writing tools, to a designer of "plan-o-gram" software used by stores to maximize their use of shelf space. . . .
>
> These deals . . . put Oracle in a small club of cash-rich companies bargain-hunting amid the worst economy in a generation. It's a buyer's market: As traditional sources of investment and cash gets scarcer—including, of course, paying customers—even some companies with high-quality products have turned into desperate sellers. "If I was in their shoes, I would ride it out" and try not to sell, says Sunny Singh, one of Oracle's chief dealmakers, referring to companies that have seen their valuations tumble.[4]

Oracle's acquisition of two particular companies—Skywire and Adminserver—illustrates how traditional management strategy and business cycle management strategy can fit hand in glove. From Oracle's strategic perspective, the point of these two acquisitions was to initiate a major vertical move into the insurance industry, with Skywire making software for the insurance business and AdminServer making insurance policy administration software. Because the insurance industry is heavily regulated, it offers up a fertile market for a comprehensive suite of products that touches all aspects of a company's data. Skywire and Adminserver together significantly extend Oracle's reach into this industry—and all the better that they were both acquired on the cheap.

Berkshire Hathaway Diversifies across Industries

Billionaire investor Warren Buffett's Berkshire Hathaway Inc., which today agreed to buy Constellation Energy Group Inc., is increasing the pace of deals as debt markets freeze up and stocks fall.

Buffett is making deals at a time when others can't. A yearlong contraction in global credit markets has choked funding for

*leveraged buyouts and reduced corporations' ability to acquire
rivals, shrinking the value of announced mergers 29 percent to
$2.29 trillion this year from the same period in 2007.*

—Bloomberg.com

This news excerpt highlights how, in the very midst of the chaos
and uncertainty of the crash of 2007 to 2009, Warren Buffett and
his Berkshire Hathaway company went on a buy-low spending spree
with an even broader strategic focus than Oracle. In Buffett's case,
his Master Cyclist game has always been to spread business cycle risk
by diversifying broadly across numerous industries.

Buffett's list of diversifying acquisitions during the recent crash
was a long one. It ranged from the underwear maker Fruit of the
Loom and the auto insurer Geico to Constellation Energy, the Mars
candy bar company, and Marmon Holdings—the Pritzker family's
coterie of 125 companies.

Marubeni Diversifies across the Globe

Warren Buffett's Berkshire Hathaway was hardly the only Master
Cyclist acquirer hyperactive during the crash of 2007 to 2009.
Another big conglomerate astutely playing the same buy-low game
thousands of miles from Omaha was the Marubeni Corporation,
one of Japan's largest conglomerates. In fact, Marubeni played the
crash like a virtuoso.

In strategic preparation for its acquisitions concerto, Marubeni
began to build up its cash position beginning in 2006 both through
its own organic growth as well as through the divestiture of a
number of subsidiaries that were operating in highly cyclical industries. Once the crash hit, Marubeni then used its large cash position
to purchase a large set of energy companies, agricultural firms, and
alternative energy businesses in North America and Europe. It also
acquired professional service firms in Asia.

Through these acquisitions, Marubeni was not only seeking to
spread risk across a variety of industries like Berkshire Hathaway.
It was also reinforcing a strong global diversification in its business
model.

Whether all of the strategic acquisitions of companies such as
Berkshire Hathaway, Marubeni, and Oracle will ultimately be accretive

to earnings remains to be seen. However, one Always a Winner point should be abundantly clear: If you conserve your cash and are patient during the bullish upward trend of the stock market cycle, you will be loaded for bear once a bear market hits.

Action Item

Review your organization's acquisition and divestiture activity over the last decade. Based on your organization's behavior, has it acted like a Master Cyclist or a Reactive Cyclist in this dimension? If you are contemplating any new acquisitions, have you considered what portion of the stock market cycle we are likely in now?

How to Minimize Your Capital Financing Costs over the Interest Rate Cycle

Shave a couple of hundred basis points off your capital costs over the course of the business cycle and save your organization millions of dollars. That's the mind-set every Master Cyclist brings to the capital financing table.

In this critical Always a Winner dimension, corporate finance teams have at least two parameters to optimize: the organization's debt-to-equity ratio and its ratio of short-term to long-term debt. Both of these parameters change over the course of the business cycle and the related stock market and interest rate cycles. Only by strategically exploiting these cyclical changes in the debt-to-equity and short-term to long-term debt ratios over time will your capital financing costs truly be minimized.

OPTIMIZING YOUR DEBT-TO-EQUITY RATIO

While stock and bond returns largely move together over the business cycle, the relative costs of equity and debt significantly differ over the cycle.[1] This fact is evident in Exhibit 22.1, which contrasts the total return[2] of the Standard & Poor's 500 stock market index with the total return of the Barclays U.S. Aggregate Bond Index.[3]

You can see in this exhibit that stock market returns are generally higher than bond returns. These higher equity returns reflect

Exhibit 22.1   Stock versus Bond Returns over Time

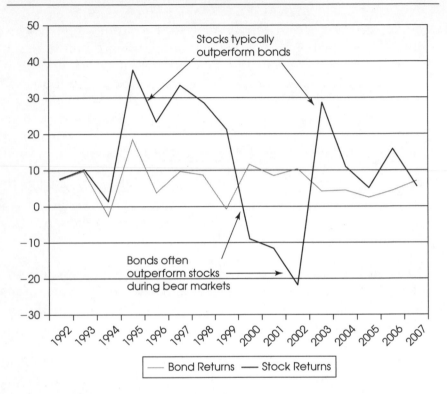

a higher degree of risk—bond payments are more certain because bond investors have a prior claim to the assets of a firm relative to shareholders.

However, in the exhibit, you can also see that the spread between stock market and bond market returns continually narrows and widens over the course of the business cycle. Moreover, at certain times during the business cycle and the related stock market and bond market cycles, *bond returns can be significantly higher than stock returns.*

For example, when the business cycle turns down, stock prices drop significantly, and the stock market falls into a downward bearish trend, with bonds often outperforming stocks. Just look at the interval from 2000 to 2002 in the exhibit, which spans a vicious bear market. The superior performance of bonds succinctly illustrates why it can be so very useful to alter your organization's debt-to-equity ratio over the course of the business cycle.

As for how to play the debt-to-equity ratio optimizing game, consider that in the mid- and late stages of a business cycle expansion, the stock market is typically in a strong upward bullish trend. At such times, the "currency" of an organization's stock price is at its strongest. At such times, it is therefore far better to fund new expenditures—for instance, the acquisition of a rival—through the issuance of new stock shares rather than by taking on new debt. This is all the more true because during the mid- to late stages of an economic expansion, interest rates typically are rising in the related interest rate cycle along with stock prices.

Conversely, when the stock market has entered a downward bearish trend, interest rates are likely to fall, and debt is likely to be relatively cheaper. At such times, it is better to rely relatively more on debt than equity.

In addition, many organizations find that buying back stock during bear markets at a depressed price can yield a very high return on that investment. Using company cash to reacquire equity shares when they are undervalued not only helps provide more value to the remaining shareholders; it also helps support the company's stock price.

Broadcom Finances with Equity, Conexant Loads Up on Debt

One of my favorite illustrations of the strategic use—and misuse—of equity financing versus debt financing over the course of the business cycle is offered by the diverging paths of two cross-town rivals in Orange County, California: Broadcom and Conexant. Both of these semiconductor companies engaged in aggressive acquisition programs leading up to the 2001 recession, and, contrary to the buy-low Master Cyclist dictum, both paid premium prices for their acquisitions.

However, on the Master Cyclist side, Broadcom primarily used equity financing and its own high-priced stock to finance its acquisitions. In contrast, the Reactive Cyclist Conexant used heavy debt financing. Predictably, when the recession hit, Conexant was all but crushed by its debt obligations and turned into a penny stock while Broadcom was able to weather the storm—its overpriced acquisitions notwithstanding.

OPTIMIZING YOUR SHORT- TO LONG-TERM DEBT RATIO

It is not just that the cost of debt relative to equity changes over the course of the business cycle and the related stock market and interest rate cycles. So, too, does the cost ratio of short-term to long-term debt.

This immutable law of bond market dynamics is clearly visible in Exhibit 22.2. This exhibit compares short-term interest rates on Triple-A commercial paper to the long-term rates on Triple-A 10-year corporate bonds.

In this exhibit, you can see that during those periods in which the spread is the widest between the two rates—for example, in areas labeled A and B in the exhibit—it is better to rely more on relatively cheaper short-term debt. During such periods, organizations can

Exhibit 22.2   Ever-Changing Relationship between Short-Term and Long-Term Interest Rates

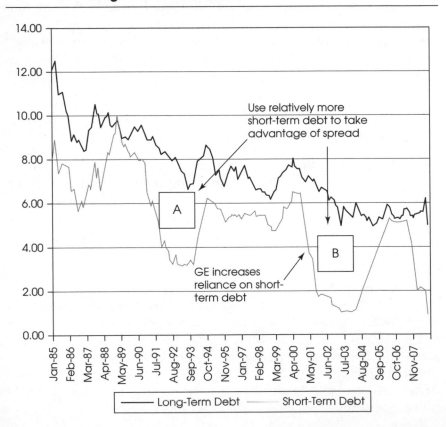

cut their interest rate expenses by refinancing some of the organization's long-term debt with short-term financing. It is equally advantageous to use short-term financing for ongoing capital expenditures as a bridge to a period in which long-term rates will once again fall.

When the spread is relatively narrow between short- and long-term rates and rates are relatively low, that can be a good opportunity to lock in low long-term rates and thereby reduce strains on cash flow.

Two cases—one with considerable controversy—help illustrate the dynamics of optimizing the short- to long-term debt ratio to reduce financing costs.

GE Gets Roundly—and Wrongly—Criticized by the "Bond King"

In the wake of the September 11, 2001, terrorist attack, Federal Reserve chairman Alan Greenspan orchestrated a historic reduction in short-term interest rates. In fact, the Fed Funds rate was cut to near zero, making short-term money as close to free as it ever gets. Meanwhile, as you can see in Exhibit 22.2 during the interval marked by area B, the spread between short and long-term debt significantly widened.

During this interval, one of the companies that astutely and aggressively increased its reliance on short-term debt to take advantage of low short-term interest rates and the widened spread was General Electric. In fact, GE increased its short-term debt to over $100 billion worth of commercial paper—an amount more than three times the normal rate (as measured by its bank line coverage).

For its efforts to minimize its financing costs, GE got roundly—and quite wrongly—criticized by the so-called Bond King of Wall Street, Bill Gross. Bill Gross is the managing director of PIMCO, which runs the largest bond fund in the world; and when the Bond King speaks, he can move the stock price of a company sharply up or down with the same power as other luminaries such as Warren Buffett.

In this case, Gross wrongly accused GE and its chairman, Jeff Immelt, of using too much short-term debt to fund too many acquisitions. In fact, what GE primarily was doing was seeking to minimize its interest expenses during a period in which Immelt and his finance team correctly assumed that there would be no risk of any upward spike in short-term rates.

An example offered up in one of Bill Gross's very own newsletters illustrates the savings to be had by GE. Gross observed that if you move $11 billion from 6-1/2% long term debt to short term 1-3/4% commercial paper, that's a savings in annual interest expenses of about $500 million!

For Immelt's efforts to cut GE's interest expenses, GE shareholders were nonetheless severely punished by the Bond King. On the day that Gross made his intemperate remarks, GE shares fell by fully 6%—a huge move for a blue-chip stock. This is a cautionary tale of what can happen when a bond expert tries to manage somebody else's company through the media.

Wachovia Leverages the Spread

Another cautionary tale, a tale concerning the now-fallen Wachovia, helps us conclude this chapter. Once America's fourth-largest financial institution, Wachovia fell on its sword during the crash of 2007 to 2009. As we saw in Chapter 21, Wachovia's disastrous buy-high purchase of Golden West Financial doomed it to a shotgun marriage with Wells Fargo.

This fatal miscue notwithstanding, Wachovia's executive team was not without its Master Cyclist virtues, at least during the 2001 recession. At that time, Wachovia strategically leveraged its short- to long-term interest rate spread even as it synergistically changed its product mix. On the spread issue, as the 2001 recession took hold and interest rates began to fall, Wachovia significantly increased its short-term to long-term debt ratio. This alone shaved millions of dollars off the company's debt costs.

In addition, with default risk rising, Wachovia decreased the total amount it had committed to unsecured loans and thereby increased its total dollar deposits. Wachovia thus was able to fund additional mortgage products with these increased deposits while mitigating risk.[4]

It is important to cite Janus-faced cases like Wachovia because its 2001 success juxtaposed against its crash-and-burn strategic miscues leading up to the crash of 2007 to 2009 reiterates one of the most important findings of my research:

> Companies that do well in some areas of Master Cyclist management often perform abysmally in other areas.

This insight underscores the critical importance of more broadly building a Master Cyclist organization with an appropriate structure, culture, degree of economic and financial market literacy, and forecasting capability. Accordingly, this insight provides a natural segue to the final part of this book, where we will learn more precisely how to build the Master Cyclist organization. By building such an organization, your organization can be Always a Winner.

Action Item

Carefully review your organization's debt-to-equity ratio over the last decade. Has your corporate finance team attempted to fine-tune that ratio to minimize its capital cost? Did your organization ever overburden itself with high-cost long-term debt that created significant cash flow problems during recessions?

Conduct a similar analysis of your organization's short- to long-term debt ratio. Did your organization's finance team take advantage of historically low short-term interest rates during the last two recessions to refinance its long-term debt?

STEP III

BUILDING THE ALWAYS
A WINNER ORGANIZATION

23

Why Always a Winner Organizations Always Begin with a Strong Business Cycle Management Orientation

We all know the cliché—and we all know the going's been tough for a lot of companies in the past two years. Economies in recession. Sales flat. Confidence in American business down. So for years, we've been doing what Caterpillar people always do in tough times. Going. Leading. Responding. Adjusting. Adapting. Doing what it takes to keep our company strong and profitable. . . . Because tough times or not, this company just keeps getting stronger, better and tougher all the time.

—Caterpillar 2002 Annual Report

Thus far in this book, we have armed ourselves with a powerful set of forecasting tools with which to anticipate movements and key turning points in the business cycle. Learning these forecasting skills was Step One in the strategic business cycle management process

In Step Two, we learned to apply a very powerful set of battle-tested strategies and tactics over the course of the business cycle in response to our forecasting data. We also learned that it is through the application of such strategies and tactics that true Always a Winner organizations find competitive advantage relative to rivals in an up-and-down economy and thereby achieve superior performance.

Now, in Step Three, one more critical task lies before us. For you to engage in truly effective strategic business cycle management over the many different functional areas of the organization and over the longer term, it is critical that you learn to rebuild your organization to reflect its new strategic intent.

In this regard, the reigning authority on both the necessity and virtue of organizations adapting to reflect their changing strategy is the noted Harvard Business School historian Alfred Chandler. In his classic book *Strategy and Structure,* Chandler astutely noted that structure must always follow strategy.[1]

The many scholars who have followed in Chandler's erudite wake highlight the importance not just of a firm's organizational structure but also its culture and broader strategic orientation as well as the defining characteristics of its executive team.

Following in this rich scholarly tradition and through the benefit of hundreds of case studies, I have learned that to become a truly effective strategic business cycle manager, an organization needs to possess these four characteristics:

1. A strong business cycle management orientation
2. An executive team that is highly literate about macroeconomics and the financial markets
3. An organizational structure that facilitates the flow of forecasting data and timely decision making
4. An organizational culture that supports business cycle management activities

In this chapter, we focus on the first characteristic—the overriding importance of a strong business cycle management orientation. Then in the next three chapters we sequentially tackle the topics of executive team literacy, a facilitative organizational structure, and a supportive organizational culture.

WHAT IS A BUSINESS CYCLE MANAGEMENT ORIENTATION?

Great companies plan for, and prosper through, all economic cycles.

—Richard Priory, CEO, Duke Energy

This quotation perfectly captures the essence of a business cycle management orientation in Always a Winner companies and leaders. The term *business cycle management orientation* refers to the recognition of the organization's executive team that recessions represent not only potentially extreme dangers. More broadly, movements and key turning points in the business cycle represent potential sources of competitive and sustainable advantages as well as important determinants of both the flow and stability of future earnings.

In fact, the incredible strategic opportunities that cyclical downturns present are always uppermost in the minds of executives such as Teruo Asada, president and chief executive of Marubeni, Japan's fifth-largest trading company. His mantra is simply: "Hard times often come hand in hand with opportunities."[2]

In many ways, the opportunities that Always a Winner executives like Asada seek to capitalize on come about through a classic Darwinian struggle where only the fittest survive during a recession. This Darwinian struggle is evident in the words of Dan DiMicco, the chairman of Nucor Steel, who notes: "We intend to take advantage of the economic downturn to gain market share, penetrate new markets, and emphasize cost reductions."[3]

Because of the strategic opportunities inherent in movements of the business cycle, executive teams with a strong business cycle management orientation are outwardly focused on broader macroeconomic events. These teams seek a continuous inflow of information from various forecasting resources, suppliers, and customers. In this way, a business cycle orientation helps the organization forecast future demand for both resource planning and strategic purposes.

In this process, every executive team with a strong business cycle management orientation fully understands the intimate connection between the trajectory of the economy and a firm's bottom line. As the chief financial officer of Arden Realty once succinctly put it: "The monitoring of the health of the economy is essential to our success."[4]

Beyond an overriding awareness of business cycle movements and the strategic opportunities that recessions in particular present, a strong business cycle orientation also emphasizes this critical point:

> Truly effective strategic business cycle management is ultimately a learning process based on an organization's cumulative experience with dealing with past adversity.

Because it learned from past recessions, the former "tractor" company Caterpillar became much more diversified and business cycle savvy. As a result, its executive team can now boast, as it did in the 2002 Annual Report: "We are no longer a victim of the same business cycles we experienced in the past."

As to why past recessions can be such a transformative learning tool for the business cycle–oriented organization, Leonard Jaskol, the former chief executive and chairman of Lydall, offers this compelling metaphor:

> Recessions teach companies to be prepared even during the good times, because a recession is like a battle—when you're in it, it's almost too late to start training for it; if you're not prepared for it, you will pay for it.

WHY A STRONG BUSINESS CYCLE MANAGEMENT ORIENTATION MATTERS

One of the most important reasons why a strong business cycle management orientation matters may be found in one of the most important and powerful conclusions of my Master Cyclist Project research:

> Even if some organizations are able to strategically manage the business cycle in some functional areas of the corporation, such as marketing or human resources, these organizations may *not* be able to transfer those business cycle management skills to other functional areas of the firm, such as corporate finance or supply chain management.

This conclusion may at first seem counterintuitive. After all, if an organization is good at managing the business cycle in one area, shouldn't it be good at managing in other areas?

In fact, the inability of many organizations to transfer strategic business cycle management skills across their functional areas is a problem fully consistent with the academic literature on the difficulties of knowledge transfer within organizations.[5] This problem is also fully consistent with the well-known functional silo structure of most corporations that helps wall off the different functions from each other.

From an academic perspective, such compartmentalized, silo-like behavior clearly fits the pattern of localized learning described by Richard Cyert and James March. These famous Carnegie Mellon professors found strong evidence that firms respond to problems identified in a particular area by searching for solutions in that area. However, these firms may not be able to generalize that solution to other areas of the firm.[6]

In a strategic business cycle management context, a firm thus may search for a solution to the excess inventories that often accumulate during a recession. This search may, in turn, lead to more sophisticated inventory management that will lead to better inventory control in the next recession. It doesn't necessarily follow, however, that the lessons and techniques learned in the supply chain management shop will transfer over to the marketing and human resources departments.

A classic case in point involves the high-tech Internet router king Cisco Systems. After Cisco's executive team had to write down the value of its inventories by more than $2 billion during the 2001 recession, the company's supply chain managers moved to a more business cycle–sensitive, real-time supply chain management system. These reforms do not appear, however, to have permeated across the whole corporation.

In fact, the case study research of the Master Cyclist Project abounds with examples of companies that successfully executed business cycle management strategies in one functional area of the firm but failed miserably in other areas.

The case of Wachovia in Chapter 22 aptly demonstrated this point. Other companies that have successfully executed Master Cyclist strategies during the 2001 recession but that stumbled badly managing through the crash of 2007 to 2009 include the world's cement king Cemex, the once-proud and mighty Countrywide Financial, and KB Home.[7] What all of these companies ultimately lacked was a strong business cycle management orientation to carry them through multiple turns of the business cycle.

CHAPTER 24

How Every Executive Team Can Boost Its Economic and Financial Market Literacy

Over the last 20 years, I have taught thousands of executive MBA students and addressed thousands more top executives in a wide variety of public forums. During this time, I have never failed to be astonished by the widespread lack of economic and financial market literacy among a significant fraction of America's executive corps.

This is hardly a subjective assessment. At the beginning of my executive MBA classes and before I even begin teaching my classes on macroeconomics and managing the business cycle, I regularly benchmark my students with an economic and financial market literacy test. This objective test consists of relatively simple questions about basic macroeconomic principles, such as the difference between fiscal and monetary policy, the relationship between inflation and interest rates, and the difference between cost-push versus demand-pull inflation. Invariably, many of the scores logged by the students—many of them top executives at their companies—are far closer to the 50% flunking range than the 100% A range.

I also get the very same "lack of literacy" result when I speak before large corporate audiences—even when I speak to highly sophisticated groups of investors or chief executive officers. Again, this is not a subjective judgment.

To measure economic and financial market literacy objectively at these speeches, I regularly use an audience response system that allows me to poll the audience on such concepts as the difference between leading and lagging economic indicators, the relationship between bond prices and bond yields, and the difference between fixed and floating exchange rates—all concepts that must be understood in order to properly manage either money or companies over the course of the business cycle. Invariably, many participants score quite low on the literacy scale.

WHAT ACCOUNTS FOR AMERICA'S LOW LEVEL OF LITERACY?

Over many years, I've thought a lot about this problem of the low level of economic and financial market literacy within America's executive corps. In fact, the existence of this problem is just one of the many reasons why I sat down to write this book. My strong view is that if the United States is going to prosper over the longer term, it is critical that its executives have a much more sophisticated understanding of the business cycle and, more broadly, international economics and finance.

As to why there is a relatively low level of macroeconomic and financial market literacy among the American executive corps, I believe there are several important factors at work. One such factor is the relative lack of business cycle volatility during the formative years of many of America's top executives.

In this regard, many of the older top executives running companies in today's turbulent times were young men and women in middle management positions during the 1990s. This was a decade in which America had the longest economic expansion in its history; and these halcyon days were the executives' formative years.

Unfortunately, the lack of significant business cycle volatility during this halcyon period significantly reduced the executives' incentives to learn about the business cycle—and they are now paying a very heavy price. Of course, today, the situation is exactly reversed. Now there is a great hunger for a deeper understanding of the extremely volatile macroeconomic environment within which businesses operate.

A second major factor that accounts for a general lack of economic and financial market literacy is the failure of MBA education in this country. Here the problem is that many of America's top business schools don't even require the teaching of macroeconomics in their core curriculum. This problem is further compounded by the dominance of corporate finance departments at most major business schools and the prevailing random-walk dogma that most corporate finance professors still myopically cling to—despite a mountain of evidence that both the business cycle and the stock market can be forecast and managed.

HOW TO RAISE AMERICA'S LITERACY BAR

Regardless of why far too many members of America's business executive corps may be characterized by a relatively low level of economic and financial market literacy, it is critical that the literacy bar be raised. To raise this bar requires both a commitment to the daily discipline of reading the financial press and a longer-term commitment to training programs that systematically upgrade the business cycle management skills of the executive team.

In reading the financial press, it is essential for every business executive to very *quickly* and *intelligently* read at least three newspapers a day: the *Wall Street Journal,* the *Financial Times,* and *Investor's Business Daily.* I also recommend a weekly read of the *Economist* for the latest in global financial news. (I don't mean to diminish the importance of other fine publications, such as *BusinessWeek, Forbes, Fortune,* and so on. I'm just suggesting one way busy managers can conduct a financial press triage.)

With regard to my required reading publications, the *Wall Street Journal* is the preeminent financial newspaper in the United States. The *Financial Times,* which is a U.K. newspaper, provides a more global perspective of the international financial and economic news. Together with the weekly *Economist,* also from the United Kingdom, these news publications are essential reading in today's global business environment.

As for *Investor's Business Daily,* this newspaper will help you parse the economic news more specifically through the lens of the financial markets. Its "Big Picture" daily column is worth the price of the subscription alone; it provides a succinct analysis of how the day's economic news may have moved the financial markets.

Read Quickly and Intelligently!

Now please note that I didn't just say to read these publications. I said to read them both "very quickly" and "intelligently." These two distinctions are extremely important.

By "very quickly," I mean that you need not read every word of every article in every section of these publications. Rather, your goal should be to skim them quickly and read more closely only those articles that are germane to the mission of managing your company and, more broadly, the business cycle. This means you must learn to skim these newspapers with an eagle eye and an ability to focus in a laserlike fashion on articles that may be of particular interest.

For example, in my own daily discipline of reading these publications, it takes me no more than 20 minutes a day. That would seem to be a reasonable standard as I am by no means a speed reader.

Now, what do I mean by reading these publications "intelligently"? This is also a very interesting distinction.

In my own experience teaching top executives in my MBA classes, it has become clear that many who regularly read the financial press do so without a complete understanding of what they are reading. The central problem is that these executives may think they know exactly what is going on in the story. However, when pressed to explain a story in my classroom, many have difficulty doing so. To see what I mean, consider this short and seemingly simple passage from a story that appeared in the *Financial Times* about the possibility that the Arab state of Qatar in the Middle East might depeg its currency from the dollar.

> Qatar is reviewing its currency policy and could revalue or drop the dollar peg as the booming Gulf state struggles to tame inflation while the US reduces interest rates to head off a recession. . . . Qatar is constrained in its fight against inflation because the dollar peg forces it to track US monetary policy.[1]

On the surface, this does indeed seem like a pretty simple passage. But how exactly would dropping the dollar peg help Qatar fight inflation? And why does the dollar peg force the Qatar's central bank to "track US monetary policy"? To answer these questions—and to understand the broader strategic implications of this story for your organization—you actually have to know quite a bit of macroeconomics.

For starters, you have to understand the difference between fixed and floating exchange rates, how countries with fixed exchange rates maintain their pegs, and, of course, just what a peg is. You also must understand that when the Federal Reserve cuts interest rates in the United States, foreign capital tends to leave the United States for places like Qatar, and such foreign investment tends to drive up the value of Qatar's currency. To counter this upward pressure, Qatar's central bank will have to match the interest rate cuts of the Federal Reserve with interest rate cuts of its own.

Note, however, that in the process of making these interest rate cuts, Qatar will, in effect, be increasing its money supply. This increase in its money supply will, in turn, increase domestic demand and thereby create inflationary pressures. This is why Qatar often hates it when the United States Federal Reserve cuts interest rates. It is also why Qatar is being forced to reevaluate its fixed peg policy.

On top of all of this, to parse the implications of this story completely, it would also be useful to know that in order to maintain the dollar peg, Qatar would likely have to take many of the export dollars it earns from the United States through the sale of oil and recycle those dollars back into the U.S. bond market. In this way, Qatar bids up the price of the dollar in international exchange markets and thereby helps maintain its own peg.

Of course, when Qatar buys U.S. Treasury bonds to maintain its dollar peg, this helps keep interest rates low in America. This is because Qatar's increased demand for U.S. bonds drives up bond prices. Because bond prices are inversely related to bond yields, Qatar's purchase of U.S. bonds therefore helps push down bond yields and interest rates. And by the way, because world oil prices are denominated in dollars, when the U.S. Federal Reserve cuts interest rates, this also drives up oil prices. However, when pegging its currency to the dollar, Qatar doesn't really benefit from this spike in oil prices because the spike is offset by the falling value of its currency.

Now, if you knew all of these things in reading this passage, it would soon become very apparent why a small little story on the back pages of the *Financial Times* might have a very big impact on the management of your company. In particular, if Qatar and other oil-rich Gulf states were to abandon the dollar peg and allow their currency to float, this would simultaneously cause the dollar to plunge, interest rates in the United States to spike, and oil prices to fall.

If your organization is in a capital-intensive industry that requires large amounts of borrowing, this spike in interest rates from Qatar's depegging would put a severe cramp in your organization's ability to access low cost capital. If, however, your company depends on selling exports to the rest of the world for its livelihood, this plunge in the dollar would be good news because it would improve your competitive advantage in the international marketplace.

The broader point I'm trying to make here is that the daily financial press is chock full of clues about coming business cycle and economic trends that may affect your organization's bottom line. Only if you are able to understand the broader economic and financial context within which these clues appear will you be able to make the appropriate forecasts, draw the appropriate conclusions, and apply the appropriate business cycle management strategies. The key to being able to do all of this is boosting your own economic and financial market literacy.

UPGRADING YOUR ORGANIZATION'S LITERACY

Beyond changing your individual behavior to cultivate the daily discipline of reading the financial press, it is critical that your organization take appropriate steps to both share economic insights among executive team members and upgrade the literacy of the executive team. It follows that both formal weekly meetings and informal discussions to discuss the emerging economic news from a strategic perspective should be a staple of your organization's regular calendar. In an asynchronous world increasingly dominated by Internet communication, a healthy flow of e-mail correspondence on economic and financial market issues is likewise desirable.

In terms of upgrading the literacy of your organization and its executive team, I also strongly recommend regular training programs to enhance economic education. These programs can be conducted in-house—the teachers and trainers can come to you. Alternatively, your organization may want to develop a relationship with a local business school to provide such executive education.

Regardless of how you go about boosting the economic and financial market literacy of your organization, these are just a few of the things that every business cycle management strategist should be able understand:

- How fiscal and monetary policies work
- The possible effects of open market operations by the Federal Reserve on foreign investment flows, long-term interest rates, and currency values
- The critical relationships among productivity, growth, and inflation
- The differences among leading, lagging, and coincident indicators
- Why the stock market is a leading indicator of the business cycle
- Why the bond market's yield curve is one of the best forecasting tools available
- How trade deficits reduce economic growth and jobs in the deficit country
- Why oil price shocks, Federal Reserve rate hikes, a falling stock market, and a flattening yield curve all provide strong, albeit imperfect, signals of recession

Action Item

If you do not already do so, subscribe to the *Wall Street Journal*, the *Financial Times, Investor's Business Daily*, and the *Economist* and begin the daily discipline of reading these publications. If you are a chief executive of an organization, make the decision to provide free subscriptions of these publications to all members of your top management team. In addition, provide free copies of these publications in all public areas where managers congregate, such as the coffee room and the cafeteria. More broadly, explore training programs for your organization that can be administered either in-house or through your local business school.

25

Why a Facilitative Structure Must Follow Your Business Cycle Management Strategy

Strategy is based on matching opportunities and capabilities. Capabilities reside in a firm's shared know-how, and firm structure serves to mobilize a firm's capabilities in pursuit of opportunities.

—Professors David Baron and David Besanko

This astute observation aptly underscores the critical relationship between a firm's organizational structure and its implementation of various strategies.[1] The question before us in this chapter is just what *kind* of structure must your organization develop to strategically manage the business cycle effectively and efficiently over the longer term. The answer may be found in three specific structural dimensions.

1. Your organizational structure must facilitate the timely acquisition, processing, and dissemination of forecasting information. This information must flow freely and swiftly both

vertically up and down the chain of command and *horizontally* across the many functional areas of the firm. To put this dimension most simply:

> An accurate forecast is only as good as the managers that it reaches.

2. Your organizational structure must facilitate the equally timely, synergistic, and integrative implementation of strategic business cycle management principles. In many cases, this will require tearing down the functional silo walls that characterize most organizations.
3. Both your forecasting and strategy-setting capabilities must be integrated across the firm and not segregated in separate shops far from the centers of power and command.

GETTING YOUR VERTICAL DIMENSION RIGHT

Vertically, your organization must be structured so that all available information related to both forecasting the business cycle and strategically managing that cycle can move freely and swiftly both up and down the chain of command—from the shop floor to the executive suite and back again. The failure to eliminate organizational friction in this vertical dimension often means the failure to act in a timely way on what might otherwise be quite accurate forecasting information within your organization's own borders.

We have already seen this problem of trapped information briefly illustrated in the case of the once-high-flying chip maker Conexant. A more detailed recounting of this story is critical to understanding the importance of a facilitative organizational structure.

Conexant's Middle Managers Get Trapped in a Cone of Silence

In the months leading up to the 2001 recession, middle managers at Conexant's supply chain management shop saw that inventories at the company's distributor locations and in Taiwan were going up, that wafer supplies were becoming plentiful in Asia as capacity factors were going down, and that customers were no longer complaining if an order was shipped a few days late.

While these internally observed industry indicators all strongly signaled that both the business cycle and semiconductor cycle were turning down, Conexant's top management team nevertheless did not act on this information. Instead, the top team embraced a much rosier forecast and then locked the company into very costly take-or-pay deals with suppliers predicated on what would turn out to be its overly optimistic forecasts.

Ironically, when the company experienced large losses, Conexant's chief executive officer blamed it on "the deepest, most abrupt business reversal in the history of the semiconductor industry"—seemingly oblivious to the warning signs emanating from within his own company. In fact, the real culprit in Conexant's dismal performance over the course of the recession was an organizational structure that lacked adequate communications channels across the various layers of management and an overly centralized decision-making process that ignored vital information from its own functional areas.[2]

GETTING YOUR HORIZONTAL DIMENSION RIGHT

Horizontally, your organization must be structured so that all available information related to both forecasting the business cycle and strategically managing that cycle can flow equally freely and swiftly across the various functional areas of the firm—from marketing, human resources management, and capital finance, to supply chain management, mergers and acquisitions, and risk management. Unfortunately, far too many organizations are horizontally structured as walled functional silos that report to a top management team. These functional silo walls, which often are quite high and unscalable, significantly impede the horizontal flow of information across functions and doom an organization to business cycle management failure—even when some functional areas of the organization are quite skilled at managing the business cycle.

To see the problem, consider a typical organizational chart in which a CEO oversees a set of separate boxed functions organized horizontally next to one another. Across these boxes, Jack runs the human resources management department. Jill runs the production department. Jorge is in charge of mergers and acquisitions. And so it goes across the various functional areas.

This kind of organizational structure may make sense for any number of reasons. However, these high-walled functional silos not only prevent the synergistic and integrative application of strategic business management principles across the organization. They also drastically impede the transfer of business cycle management skills and knowledge across the functional areas.

Consider the problem of synergy. Even if the supply chain management shop accurately foresees a recession on the horizon and begins to ramp down its production, a very fast-moving recession still may lead to unwanted inventory buildups. In such cases, the marketing department could pitch in and help trim these unwanted inventories with a set of price promotions and increased advertising. However, if the two departments arrayed horizontally on the organizational chart are not used to working together on business cycle management issues, this coordination of Master Cyclist strategy is unlikely to happen.

An even bigger problem with the functional silo organizational structure is that the highly valuable strategic business cycle management skills and knowledge of one unit, such as finance or accounting, may not be readily transferred to other functional areas, such as marketing or human resources management. Time and time again, in my case study research, I have seen precisely this problem. As my colleague Phil Bromiley has trenchantly noted:

> "Companies that may excel in one area of strategic business cycle management often fail miserably in others. This is because high functional silo walls have prevented the appropriate skill and knowledge transfer."

Only by breaking down your organization's functional silo walls will you be able to strategically manage the business cycle across the entire organization.

INTEGRATE! DON'T SEGREGATE!

The third major structural characteristic of the Always a Winner organization is a set of integrative, rather than segregated, forecasting and strategic management capabilities. All too often, the economic forecasting shop is tucked away in some far dark corner of some faraway building, and the members of that forecasting team have little or no access to the top executive suites or the managers running the various departments. Isolating the forecasting team creates an "out of sight, out of mind" problem even as it limits forecasting team access to decision makers.

A similar problem arises with the strategy function. Here, again, many companies view the formulation and implementation of strategy as a separate and segregated function rather than an integrative one. In such organizations, the strategy team may fail to elicit the appropriate amount of coordination and support from the various functional units.

DuPont Offers a Structural Archetype

One company that never makes this kind of mistake, and that has learned over time to build an organizational structure that facilitates its strategic business cycle management activities, is the chemical giant DuPont.

In fact, DuPont is one of very few major corporations that still maintains its own team of economists. It has also built an extensive set of forecasting models, has very formal channels of communication across its business units to process and disseminate the information, regularly communicates to shareholders the role of the business cycle in determining earnings performance, and is led by a management team with the clear authority to respond quickly to the onset of a new business cycle event.

Perhaps not coincidentally, DuPont tends to perform well over all phases of the business cycle—despite the highly cyclical nature of its operations. Perhaps not surprisingly, it was one of the few major corporations in America that could issue a statement like this during the depths of the 2007–2009 crash:

> DuPont begins 2009 with a strong balance sheet after delivering $3.1 billion cash from operations and $1.1 billion in free cash flow in 2008. DuPont's strong balance sheet provides us with ample liquidity and low funding cost, which is a source of competitive advantage [and] the company is well-positioned beyond the recession and confident in its long-term growth strategies, which remain intact.[3]

The bottom line in this chapter is that building an organizational structure that is fully capable of supporting your strategic business cycle forecasting and management activities is absolutely critical to the long-term success of your organization. Time spent on this critical task will be time very well spent indeed.

Action Item

Conduct your own organizational structure analysis based on the checklist implied by this chapter.

Determine whether strategic business cycle management information can flow freely up and down the chain of command and across the functional areas.

Identify ways to improve this flow.

Assess whether your organization has segregated or integrated its forecasting and strategy teams.

26

Why a Supportive Organizational Culture Is Essential to Always Being a Winner

Co-founder Gordon Moore came up with three rules of recessions that have become ingrained in Intel's culture. They are: Economic downturns always end. Some companies emerge from recessions stronger than before. You can't save your way out of a recession.

—BusinessWeek

This passage from a feature article on the world's largest semi-conductor developer and manufacturer, Intel, helps emphasize the critical importance of an organizational culture infused with a strong awareness of the business cycle and the opportunities it presents.

A TALE OF TWO CULTURES

In fact, when it comes to cultivating a supportive organizational culture for its strategic business cycle management activities, no company does it better than Intel—except perhaps the big-rig truck manufacturer Paccar and the lowest-cost, most profitable steel company in the world, Nucor.[1]

Paccar Warns Early of the Pain

Truck manufacturer Paccar operates in one of the most cyclical of industries. Nevertheless, the company has been able to turn a profit consistently for almost 70 years. As evidence of both its business cycle orientation and its high degree of business cycle literacy, Paccar's top management team has adopted a strategy of geographically diversifying risk. Paccar's team also closely follows key industry indicators (e.g., freight tonnage) and prides itself on its almost accordionlike ability to ramp up and ramp down its production at the first sign of recovery or recession.

A major part of Paccar's nimbleness may be attributed to the company's own pragmatic and supportive organizational culture. As one assembly line operator described it: "Workers appreciate how [executives] don't go into denial or stonewall when a downswing is coming. They are frank and open about cuts, and . . . relations between the company and its unions seem to be good."[2]

To build this supportive culture from the ground up, at every new employee orientation, workers are warned that the truck business is cyclical and some layoffs are almost inevitable. It is in large part because of this early warning and frankness that once the economy recovers, loyal workers typically find their way back to Paccar's factories rather than those of the competition. In this way, Paccar's organizational culture allows it to retain much of its highly skilled workforce even though many of its members are laid off periodically. The cultural payoff: considerable savings in recruitment and training costs and its accordionlike ability to control labor costs during downturns.

Nucor Shares the Pain

Nucor has a long-standing tradition of emerging from cyclical downturns stronger than before entering them.
—Dan DiMicco, Chairman, Nucor Steel

In 1965, a company called the Nuclear Corporation was facing bankruptcy. Rather than sink into oblivion, this manufacturer of nuclear instruments and electronics reinvented itself as an innovative steelmaker and eventually renamed itself Nucor Steel.

Nucor's company-saving innovation was its pioneering embrace of "minimill" technology. Unlike traditional iron ore mills that make steel from scratch, minimills produce steel by melting recycled ferrous scrap in electric arc furnaces. Not only are the minimills smaller, less costly to build, and more efficient than traditional mills. Their smaller size and modularity allows minimills to be built closer to their customers.

Today, partly on the strength of its minimill model, Nucor rightly boasts that it is the safest, highest-quality, lowest-cost, most productive, and most profitable steel company in the world. However, what is most impressive about the company from an Always a Winner perspective is Nucor's uncanny ability to profitably navigate through the up-and-down movements of the business cycle. One important key to its success is its "share the pain" organizational culture that is every bit as innovative as its minimill technology.

With share the pain, and in direct contrast to Paccar, which quickly lays off employees as the business cycle turns down, Nucor has adopted just the opposite policy. It promises its workers there will be no layoffs. However, just like Paccar, Nucor is able to shave its labor costs during downturns; and it does so in two ways.

First, all employees—from the production line to the executive suite—willingly take pay cuts. In addition, as a morale booster for production workers, Nucor allocates the pay cuts according to a "progressive" schedule: Executives earning higher salaries take larger pay cuts on a percentage basis.

Second, all employees willingly accept cutbacks in the number of hours worked. In addition, in a strategy highlighted in Chapter 17, the company also cross-trains its workforce so that it can be shifted to other functions, such as maintenance or modernization efforts, as downturns occur. The net result is that Nucor is able to taper its labor costs very effectively and weather recessions without loss of productive capacity.

More broadly, what is so very interesting about the contrasting cases of Paccar versus Nucor is that each company possesses the very same ability to trim labor, production, and inventory costs, but this goal is achieved in a completely different fashion—with a supportive organizational culture in each company being the common thread.

The bottom line of this chapter is that culture counts big time when it comes to the a firm's bottom line over the course of the business cycle. Companies that build a business cycle orientation and awareness into the fabric of their companies reap huge dividends relative to their rivals whenever recessionary times come around—and recessions always come around.

Action Item

Evaluate your organizational culture within the context of this question: Does your organization's culture help you manage your labor and production costs during economic downturns in a way that builds up, rather than tears down, the morale of your employees? If not, how might your organizational culture be improved?

27

How to Protect Your 401(k) in an Up-and-Down Stock Market

Before we move on to the conclusion of this book, I would like to offer you this bonus chapter about how to manage your stock market investments over the course of the business cycle. At first glance, the subject of this chapter may seem tangential to the task of strategically managing the business cycle. However, what this chapter does is further illustrate the critical importance of the stock market as one of the most important leading indicators of the business cycle.

If this is not enough motivation for you as a business executive or manager to want to explore the topic of strategic money management, I would also note that it was not just small retail investors who lost more than 30% of the value of their portfolio in the 2008 market crash. Many business executives experienced similar losses to their 401(k) plans that now threaten to delay, or perhaps even derail, retirement. For these reasons, this chapter—tangential though it may initially seem—ultimately may prove to be one of the most valuable in this book.

WHY BUY-AND-HOLD INVESTORS ARE
WALL STREET'S LAMBS TO THE SLAUGHTER

While buying and holding S&P 500 Index funds worked very well during the great bull market run of the 1990's, they quickly gave up their gains during the two significant stock market declines that

followed. . . . The buy-and-hold strategy for this period produced
terrible returns.
                            —*San Francisco Business Times,* January 30, 2009

Let's begin the topic of strategically managing money over the course
of the business cycle with this pointed question: Why did so many
investors lose more than 30% of the value of their portfolio in the 2008
crash? The answer lies in the bankrupt prevailing paradigm of portfolio construction peddled by a cynical Wall Street to a gullible Main
Street—the tired and tattered investment philosophy of buy and hold.

The essence of buy and hold is that if you buy a portfolio of so-
called diversified stocks and hold them long enough, you will earn
an annual rate of return robust enough to significantly grow your
wealth and meet your retirement needs. One of the obvious flaws
in the buy and hold approach is this:

> The annual rate of return you actually will earn over time on a buy-
> and-hold portfolio is extremely sensitive to your market entry point.

On one hand, if you construct your diversified portfolio near
a market bottom at the beginning of a long bull run, you have a
pretty good chance of earning a decent return over the next 10
to 20 or 30 years. If, on the other hand, you happen to construct
your diversified portfolio near a market top and the onset of a bear
market plunge, your portfolio may spend most of its buy-and-hold
investment life simply trying to overcome its initial early losses.

The extreme sensitivity of the performance of a buy-and-hold
portfolio to its market entry point is illustrated in Exhibit 27.1. This
exhibit traces the annual stock price appreciation of the Standard
& Poor's (S&P) 500 Index. This index is used because it represents
the most broadly diversified representation of the stock market and
thus the ideal buy-and-hold portfolio for the average investor.

In the exhibit, you can see that if you had entered the market
in January 1993 at point A, just before the longest bull run in stock
market history, and held that portfolio right through January 2009

Exhibit 27.1   Why Buy-and-Hold Investing Is a Crapshoot

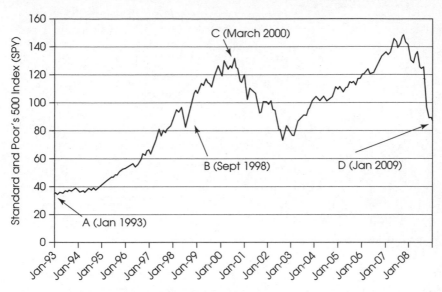

- Buy Point A, Annual Return at Point D = 11%
- Buy Point B, Annual Return at Point D = 0%
- Buy Point C, Annual Return at Point D = −4%

at point D, the buy-and-hold approach would have delivered on its promise. Specifically, you would have earned a reasonably robust return of 11% a year. That's the good news.

The bad news is that if you had entered the market well into the 1990s bull market, say during September 1998 at point B in the exhibit, your annual rate of return would have been a big fat 0% a decade later in 2008. That's obviously not the yellow brick road to a prosperous retirement.

Now for the worst news: Suppose, instead, that you had entered the market at point C in the exhibit in March 2000. If you had held on to your portfolio over the gut-wrenching roller-coaster ride of first a bear market plunge then a bull market recovery and then another bear market plunge, your annual rate of return would actually have been negative—a gut-wrenching −4% a year.

BUY AND HOLD IS ONLY A PARTIAL INSURANCE POLICY

Of course, the reason why the performance of your buy-and-hold portfolio is so sensitive to your market entry point is that, by its very design, *the buy-and-hold portfolio offers you absolutely no protection from business cycle risk*. To put this another way, by design, the traditional buy-and-hold portfolio protects you only against so-called diversifiable or unsystematic risk—not the broad market risk associated with recessionary downturns that always go hand in hand with bear markets.

Diversifiable or unsystematic risk is that risk associated with a particular *company* or with the *sector* that a company operates in. Regarding company risk, some companies simply perform worse than others because of factors such as bad management, lack of access to adequate resources, or the failure to innovate.

With sector risk, all of the companies operating in a sector or industry may fall prey to the same kind of misfortune. For example, the semiconductor industry may overbuild capacity during an economic expansion. The resultant glut of chips then forces down prices and profit margins and eventually the stock prices of chip companies—even if the economy is booming. Changes in the world trade regime, domestic tax policy, population demographics, or consumer tastes may punish or reward a particular sector and particular companies as well. For instance, despite the downturn from 2007 to 2009, the healthcare business continued to experience record growth due to the demands of the aging baby boomer population.

The buy-and-hold portfolio approach helps diversify these company- and sector-specific risks by including companies and sectors likely to move in the opposite direction from one another over time. In the typical teaching example, the buy-and-hold portfolio may have one set of holdings in the umbrella industry and another in the suntan lotion industry. Instead of holding one biotechnology stock, it may hold the whole sector in an exchange-traded fund.

Most broadly, the best way to completely diversify diversifiable risk is simply to hold the broad market, for example, by holding a mutual fund or exchange-traded fund representing the S&P 500 Index.

A BUY AND HOLD PORTFOLIO DOES NOT PROTECT YOU FROM BUSINESS CYCLE RISK!

While holding the broad market may do an excellent job of protecting your portfolio from diversifiable company and sector risks, *it does nothing whatsoever to protect you from the market risk associated with holding a portfolio through the up-and-down movements to the business cycle!* Of course, when the business cycle is in a robust upward expansionary move, so is the stock market. Under these conditions, buy-and-hold investors make out like bandits—market risk works in their favor and yields a lucrative reward.

However, when the business cycle turns down, earnings fall and stock prices fall with earnings. Under these conditions, buy-and-hold investors are severely punished by market risk, and investment returns suffer accordingly. As I noted in my book *What the Best MBAs Know:*

> [S]ystematic risk may be thought of as the risk associated with investing in the broad financial markets, for example, buying an index fund for the S&P 500. The nature of such risk is primarily cyclical. As the business cycle moves upward in an expansionary mode, the returns to the market tend to be considerably higher than the returns you to earned during downturns in the business cycle. Invariably, the years of negative returns occur during economic recessions. . . .[1]

SMART MONEY FLEECES BUY-AND-HOLD INVESTORS

Given that buy-and-hold investors always take a beating during recessions and associated bear markets, the obvious next question is this: Why doesn't Wall Street try to protect you from such market risk?

The typical answer from the dinosaurs who originally invented—and continue to defend—the buy-and-hold portfolio approach is that it is impossible to accurately forecast movements in either the business cycle or the stock market in a timely way. It follows that if you can't forecast the business cycle, then it must be futile to try to time the market by selling off your portfolio in anticipation of a recession and a collateral downward bearish move in the stock market.

Exhibit 27.2   How Wall Street Sets the Market Trend

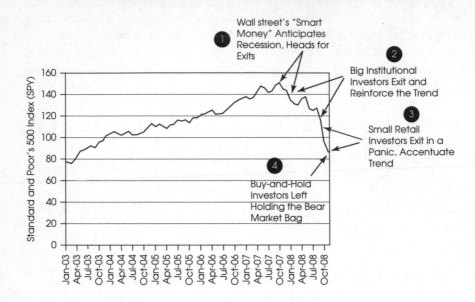

While that claim may have had considerable merit back in the heyday of the buy-and-hold philosophy during the 1950s, it is a claim that has been absolutely crushed by the weight of evidence that now supports the efficacy of the various forecasting tools you have been introduced to.

Despite strong evidence in support of the ability to forecast the business cycle accurately using the kind of leading economic indicators you have been provided in this book, the buy-and-hold philosophy remains a marketing staple of Wall Street. This philosophy remains very much in vogue largely because it allows Wall Street's "smart money" and big institutional investors to fleece Main Street's buy-and-hold investors whenever the stock market begins another downward bearish move. This fleecing process is illustrated in Exhibit 27.2.

You can see at point 1 in the exhibit that Wall Street's "smart money" is the first to head for the exits and thereby book its profits. Specifically:

When Wall Street's smart money sees a recession on the horizon, that's the time for them to get out of the market. In this way, Wall Street's smart money identifies the market top and starts the bearish downward market trend.

Wall Street's smart money knows to head for the exits because the vast majority of speculators who make up this class of investors use the same kind of forecasting tools to anticipate movements and key turning points in the business cycle that I have showed you how to use in this book.

The second stage in the progression of a bear market trend (point 2 in the exhibit) is when Wall Street's bigger institutional investors recognize sometime later in the game that the threat of recession is building. At this juncture, these bigger institutional investors will see a lot of the smart money heading for the exits. In addition, from the daily and weekly flow of the economic data, it will become increasingly obvious to these institutional investors that economic conditions are deteriorating more rapidly and that a recession is becoming more and more likely.

Of course, these big institutional investors don't dump all their holdings at once. Their holdings are simply too large to jettison in any one day without adversely affecting the prices of the very stocks they are trying to quietly dump. Instead, these big institutional investors steadily begin to sell off their holdings. As they do so, they continue to book profits while Main Street's buy-and-hold investors continue to provide their financial support for the market. In this way, through their selling action, these institutional investors help confirm the bear market trend.

In the third stage of the bear market trend (point 3 in the exhibit), as the market continues to deteriorate, small retail investors—always the last to come to the party and the last to leave—become more and more jittery. As the jitters mount, more and more of these small retail investors leave, often in a panic. This desperate selling action further accentuates, and perhaps accelerates, the downward bear market move.

Through all of this, buy-and-hold investors are the ones who take the biggest beating. It is these lambs led to the fleecing at point 4 in the exhibit who ultimately provide the smart money and big institutional investors with their capital gains.

From this description of how bear market trends develop, it should be clear that by learning how to be your own business cycle forecaster and by following stock market trends, you will not only learn how to manage your organization much better. You will become part of that small elite group of smart money and thereby manage your own money and retirement funds much better. Happy fleecing!

Concluding Thoughts

Don't play checkers in a chess world.

—Ron Vara

This book took 90 days to write and a decade to prepare for. It is the fruit of the labors of a small army of MBA students and a crack team of researchers spending thousands of hours analyzing the performance of thousands of companies, large and small, over multiple turns of the business cycle and across the globe.

Early on in this research, I quite accidentally discovered what I now believe to be the single most important set of skills and tools that managers need to navigate the turbulence of the twenty-first-century global economy. These skills and tools are all the more important because strategic business cycle management as a discipline is not regularly taught even at the very best business schools in America. That's one of the big reasons why so many managers at so many companies got caught with their bottom lines down during the crash of 2007 to 2009.

If you learn how to become your own economic forecaster, as this book teaches, you will not only develop a much better sense of the broader economic conditions within which your business operates. You will also ensure that a recession never again catches you or your organization by surprise. In addition, if you learn how to apply the set of strategic principles detailed in this book and if, over the longer term, you use the lessons of this book to build a Master Cyclist organization with the appropriate structure, culture, business cycle orientation, and level of economic literacy, your organization will almost certainly outperform any of its Reactive Cyclist rivals.

My ultimate goal in this book has been to teach you how to be Always a Winner—regardless of the economic conditions. That strategic business cycle management often trumps all other types of strategic considerations in a turbulent economy is epitomized by these words of wisdom from one of the pioneers of strategic business cycle management, Professor John McCallum:[1]

> Bets on macroeconomic direction are among the biggest enterprises make. . . . Ignoring the macroeconomy and assuming that things will continue more or less as they are doesn't mean a big bet hasn't been made.

Now that you have heard from me, I'd love to hear from you. This is particularly true if you are an executive or manager or employee or shareholder with your own story to tell about how your company managed the business cycle well—or poorly. You can reach me via my Web site, www.peternavarro.com. My very best wishes to you and yours.

PETER NAVARRO
Laguna Beach, CA
www.peternavarro.com

Notes

Chapter 2

1. Details of this case appear in Peter Navarro, *The Well-Timed Strategy* (Upper Saddle River, NJ: Wharton School Publishing, 2006), p. 116.

Chapter 3

1. Peter Navarro, "The Well-Timed Strategy: Managing the Business Cycle," *California Management Review* 48, No. 1 (2005): 10.
2. Claudia H. Deutsch, "Avon Is Sitting Pretty Despite Slow Economy," *International Herald Tribune,* June 3, 2003.
3. Navarro, "The Well-Timed Strategy," p. 13.
4. Alfred Chandler, *Strategy and Structure: Chapters in the History of the Industrial Enterprise* (Cambridge, MA: MIT Press, 1969).
5. Details of this case appear in Peter Navarro, *The Well-Timed Strategy* (Upper Saddle River, NJ: Wharton School Publishing, 2006), pp. 69–71.

Chapter 4

1. "Intel CEO On Plan to Invest & 7 billion in U.S." National Public Radio, February 10, 2009.

Chapter 6

1. The original aphorism is: "Give a man a fish and you feed him for a day. Teach a man to fish and you feed him for a lifetime."

Chapter 8

1. As a third, relatively new, option, there is the *Washington Post*-ABC News Comfort Index.

2. I prefer to use only home sales as a leading indicator of consumer durable purchases because discernible trends in the auto sales data often are distorted by the industry's frequent special marketing deals to move vehicles off the lots. I use new home sales rather than existing home sales because, in my experience, it provides a much cleaner signal of business cycle movements. This may be because even with homes, people tend to favor new things over "used" when times are good.

Chapter 10

1. www.theepochtimes.com/n2/content/view/12271.

Chapter 15

1. The Information Company, "Technology Stocks Lead Market Crash," April 15, 2005, www.domain-b.com, www.domain-b.com/investments/markets/rex_mathew/20050415_technology.htm.
2. Douglas A. McIntyre, 247WallSt.com, http://247wallst.com/2007/10/15/google-best-bel.
3. The appropriate link is http://moneycentral.msn.com/investor/market/earncalendar.

Chapter 16

1. Credit Suisse Equity Research, Advanced Micro Devices, March 5, 2009.
2. Vanessa O'Connell and Rachel Dodes, "Saks Upends Luxury Market with Strategy to Slash Prices," *Wall Street Journal,* February 13, 2009.
3. "As Saks Reports a Loss, Its Chief Offers a Plan," *New York Times,* February 26, 2009.
4. Gary McWilliams and Amy Merrick, "Retailers Sink Into the Doldrums." *Wall Street Journal,* January 18, 2008.
5. Ibid.

Chapter 17

1. "Organizational and Financial Correlates of a 'Contrarian' Human Resource Investment Strategy," *Academy of Management Review,* 35/5 (1992): 956-984, at p. 957.
2. Miguel Helft, "Layoffs across Yahoo—Finally," *New York Times,* February 12, 2008.
3. Claudia H. Deutsch, "Avon Is Sitting Pretty Despite Slow Economy," *International Herald Tribune,* June 3, 2003.
4. Ibid.
5. Peter Navarro, "The Well-Timed Strategy: Managing the Business Cycle," *California Management Review* 48, No. 1 (2005): 13.

Chapter 18

1. Peter Navarro, *The Well-Timed Strategy* (Upper Saddle River, NJ: Wharton School Publishing, 2006), pp. 98–99.
2. Peter Navarro, "The Well-Timed Strategy: Managing the Business Cycle," *California Management Review* 48, No. 1 (2005): 10.
3. Alan Ohnsman and Jeff Green, "Hyundai Defies U.S. Slump as Asians Grab Record Share," February 4, 2009.
4. Peter Valdes-Dapena, "Laid Off? Hyundai Will Take Your Car Back," CNN Money.com. January 5, 2009.
5. Navarro, "The Well-Timed Strategy."
6. Tom Ryan, "Kohl's makes grab for market share." *Wall Street Journal.* October 6, 2008.

Chapter 19

1. This case is one of my favorites. It originally appeared in Peter Navarro, *The Well-Timed Strategy* (Upper Saddle River, NJ: Wharton School Publishing, 2006), pp. 114–115.
2. Tom Ivan, "Sony: 'We Aren't Making Any Price Moves This Holiday," www .computerandvideogames.com, October 8, 2008.
3. Navarro, *The Well-Timed Strategy,* pp. 119–120.
4. Jessica Silver-Greenberg, "Discover: Credit Where Credit Is Due,"*BusinessWeek,* February 13, 2009.

Chapter 20

1. Harris's Master Cyclist astuteness notwithstanding, he still fell prey to Bernard Madoff's Ponzi scheme.
2. Chesapeake Corp. 2007 Annual Report, p. 78.
3. Peter Navarro, "Principles of the Master Cyclist," *Sloan Management* Review (2004): 23.
4. Peter Navarro, *The Well-Timed Strategy* (Upper Saddle River, NJ: Wharton School Publishing, 2006), p. 24.
5. National Public Radio, February 10, 2009 "Intel CEO on Plan to Invest $7 Billion in U.S."
6. Peter Navarro, "The Well-Timed Strategy: Managing the Business Cycle," *California Management Review* 48, No. 1 (2005): 12.
7. Mark Osborne, "Intel's Otellini Calls Bottom to Semiconductor Slump; Pulls in 32 nm Ramp." Fabtech.org/news, April 15, 2009.
8. Navarro, "Principles of the Master Cyclist."

Chapter 21

1. Peter Navarro, "The Well-Timed Strategy: Managing the Business Cycle," *California Management Review* 48, No. 1 (2005): 13.

2. Mark Mueller, "Standard Pacific's CEO Eyes Deals, Cuts Costs." *Orange County Business Journal,* January 5, 2009.
3. Ibid., p.14.
4. "Cash-Rich Oracle Scoops Up Bargains in Recession Spree," *Wall Street Journal,* February 17, 2009.

Chapter 22

1. A. Aburachis and R. Kish, "International Evidence on the Co-Movements between Bond Yields and Stock Returns: 1984–1994," *Journal of Financial & Strategic Decisions* 12, No. 2 (1999): 67–81.
2. The total return of the S&P 500 Index includes both price returns and dividend returns by adding the dividend income and price changes for a specific period. www2.standardandpoors.com/spf/xls/index/MONTHLY.xls.
3. This index represents a basket of U.S. investment-grade corporate bonds.
4. Tracy Bremmer, "Wachovia: The Monarch of Economic Prophecy," Case study, University of California-Irvine, Graduate School of Management, November 2004.

Chapter 23

1. Alfred Chandler, *Strategy and Structure: Chapters in the History of the Industrial Enterprise* (Cambridge, MA: MIT Press, 1969).
2. Yuka Hayashi, "Japanese Firms, Flush with Cash, Step Up Deals." *Wall Street Journal* January 5, 2009.
3. Peter Navarro, "The Well-Timed Strategy: Managing the Business Cycle." *California Management Review,* Vol. 48, no. 1, Fall 2005. p.5.
4. Ibid.
5. G. Szulanski, "The Process of Knowledge Transfer: A Diachronic Analysis of Stickiness," *Organizational Behavior & Human Decision Processes* 82, No. 1. (2000). 150–169.
6. Richard M. Cyert and James G. March, *A Behavioral Theory of the Firm* (Englewood Cliffs, NJ: Prentice-Hall, 1963).
7. Details of the Master Cyclist successes of these companies may be found in Peter Navarro, *The Well-Timed Strategy* (Upper Saddle River, NJ: Wharton School Publishing, 2006).

Chapter 24

1. "Qatar Considers Dropping Dollar Peg," *Financial Times,* January 30, 2008.

Chapter 25

1. D. P. Baron and D. Besanko, "Informational Alliances," *The Review of Economic Studies,* 66 (1999): 743–768, at p. 743.

2. The details of this case first appeared in Peter Navarro, "The Well-Timed Strategy: Managing the Business Cycle," *California Management Review* 48, No. 1 (2005).1–21 at p. 8.
3. "DuPont's 2009 Priorities Are Clear, says Chief Financial Officer," PR Newswire, February 10, 2009.

Chapter 26

1. The details of the Paccar and Nucor cases first appeared in Peter Navarro, "The Well-Timed Strategy: Managing the Business Cycle," *California Management Review* 48, No. 1 (2005). 1–21 at pp. 16–17.
2. Luke Timmerman, "Paccar's Rough Road," *Seattle Times*, September 24, 2000.

Chapter 27

1. Peter Navarro, *What the Best MBAs Know* (New York: McGraw-Hill, 2005), p. 205.

Concluding Thoughts

1. J. S. McCallum, "Management and the Macroeconomy," *Ivey Business Journal*, 63/3 (1999): 71–73, at p. 73.

Acknowledgements

While my name appears as the author of this book, it is in many ways a collaborative work. At the top of my list to thank at the Merage School of Business, UC-Irvine, are two of my PhD students, Greg Autry and Pedro Sottile, and one of my colleagues, Phil Bromiley.

Greg Autry is both a highly successful entrepreneur and an accomplished author in his own right. After starting up numerous successful companies, he recently returned to academia as a PhD student to devote himself full time to his research.

Over the course of the last several years, Greg has been a great sounding board, a coauthor on several occasions, and an excellent comanager of our ongoing Master Cyclist Project studying strategic business cycle management. In addition to carefully reviewing the manuscript, Greg penned the first draft of several of the cases as well as the William Stanley Jevons feature in Chapter 5. At key points in the manuscript, he also injected healthy doses of humor—a key ingredient of any book that has the words *economics, strategy,* and *business cycle* in its text.

Pedro Sottile has been working with me as a teaching assistant since joining the PhD program at the Merage School of Business. I can't say enough about his capabilities both as an award-winning performer in the classroom and as a top-notch researcher. The Master Cyclist Project, along with much of the research material derived from it, could not have flourished in the way it has without Pedro's careful stewardship. As he leaves the school next year with his newly minted PhD in finance, I hope that some top business school has the very good sense to grab him.

Phil Bromiley is the best colleague one could ever hope for. Both his door and his mind are always open, and he arrived at the Merage School of Business several years ago, just in time to provide a bridge from the copious case material of the Master Cyclist

Project to a rigorous analytical study of strategic business cycle management behavior. As one of the premier strategy scholars in the world, he literally and figuratively helped take the research up several notches to a new level.

In addition to Mssrs. Autry, Bromiley, and Sottile, I must also thank Jon Masciana and Susie Autry. Susie is Greg's "better half" and a former public school principal. Jon is a former MBA student of mine and currently the Director of Admissions and Recruiting at the Merage School. Both Jon and Susie carefully reviewed the manuscript. Jon also made a number of key contributions to the structure of the book. (The editorial help notwithstanding from my team, all errors and omissions are of course my own.)

Beyond the Merage School, there are several other people to thank for helping to bring the topic of strategic management of the business cycle into the mainstream. At the top of this list is Chris Bergonzi. A former editor at the *Sloan Management Review*, Chris worked very hard to have my first article on business cycle management published; and it was the appearance of this first article that helped lift the profile of a research stream hitherto roundly ignored in the strategy field.

I would also like to thank Professor David Vogel of the Haas School of Business at UC-Berkeley. As editor of the *California Management Review*, he oversaw a process that led to the publication of my first extended statement of the theory and practice of strategic business cycle management. This article was a finalist for the journal's prestigious annual Accenture Award, and its publication and recognition likewise helped expand the profile of the research.

At John Wiley & Sons, a big thanks to Executive Editor John DeRemigis for recruiting me for this very timely project. An equally big thanks to development editor Judith Howarth, who deftly guided the project along its very fast track.

Finally, I want to thank the cadres of MBA students who have worked on the Master Cyclist Project over the years. These students are listed below, and they range from young and very green entry-level managers to very well-seasoned CFOs and CEOS. I can't say enough about the caliber of students whom we are fortunate enough to attract at the Merage School of Business; and their excellence always makes my classroom duties a pleasure rather than a chore.

Merage Students Who Worked on Cases Related to the 2001 Recession

Keith Abercromby
Navid Alaghband
Carlos Amaya
Birju Amin
Andre Amiri
Jason Andersen
Dennis Ang
Kheng Ang
Alberto Anon
Mohammad
  Anwar
Shahbaz Anwar
Rafael Arredondo
Luke Aucoin
Russ Barlow
Robert Barrosa
Ivan Batanov
Gregory Battersby
Bret Bauer
Ramin Beizaie
Jim Bergman
Pat Blinn
Geoff Bremmer
Tracy Bremmer
Steve Brenneman
Tim Bruce
Greta Brushie
Andrew Buckland
Phiet Bui
Gabriel Cabanas
Paul Callanan
Belen Calvo
Peggy Carl
Cornel Catrina
Christen
  Chambers
Jason Chan

Frank Chen
Yi Chia Chen
David Chen
Hanwen Chen
Jeff Chen
Myron Chen
Yan Chen
Michael Chiles
Kate Choi
Simon Choi
Shun Chow
Julia Chu
Brett Clarke
Jeremy Collins
Scott Cooper
Petru Cretu
Charisma Davasia
Anthony De La
  Fuente
Rob DePrat
Sharad
  Deshpande
Keith Diehl
Ted Divon
Damon Dixon
Chad Doezie
Lisa Dolan
Richard Dragon
Ryan Dunigan
Jason Dunn
Feili Duosi
Brad Eisenstein
Francine England
Kraig Enyeart
Met Ergun
Lulu Fan
Andrew Fan

Marcello Farjalla
Mac Feller
Greg Ferrell
Gary Frazier
Rodney Fujiwara
Alejandro Fung
Jeff Furgo
Bill Georges
Luis Gomez
Maya Gowri
Jeff Greenberg
Anu Grewal
Ann Griffith
George Guerrero
Gerald Gutierrez
Miluska Gutierrez
Michael Haddadin
Todd Halbrook
May Han
Vinh Hang
Paul Harmeling
James Harris
Keith Hathaway
Jon Hawkins
Ping He
Gregory Herd
Robert Hermanson
DeAnna Hilbrants
Damian Hiley
Andrew Hill
Myra Ho
Andy Hollywood
Brian Hong
Griffin Hoover
Griff Hoover
Rezza Hosseini
Steve Houk

Chia-Chen Hu
Jennifer Hu
Jeffery Huang
Tony Huang
Raymond Ie
Jacqueline
  Interiano
John Jerney
Jerry Jew
Hao Jiang
Julie Johnson
Scott Justice
Guillermo Juvera
Mbugua Karanja
Chandrasekhar
  Karipeddi
Arvind Kaushik
Go Kawasaki
Stephanie Ke
Kevin Keegan
Rohit Khanna
Boyeon Kim
Ryan Kim
Makiko Kobayashi
Akiko Kondo
John Koontz
Bryan Koski
Ali Kowsari
Michael Krause
Jason Krupoff
Dauren
  Kylyshpekov
Mike Laird
Janak Lalan
Maria Lam
Brian Lane
Joy Langley

John Lee

Hosun Lee

Jennifer Lee

Vincenzo Lefante

Eric Li

For Li

Chang W. Lleng

Jack London

Scott Lovell

Ken Lu

Rosalind Lu

Gary Lu

Ben Luong

Anh Luu

Karen MacFarlane

Brendan Mahon

Jay Mallya

Kumar Mangalick

Donald Martens

Scott Martin

Anu Mathur

Ko Matsukubo

Josh Mauzey

Naomi McAuley

Chris McBee

Candice
  McDaniel

Punkaj Mehta

Jennifer Meissen

Scott Merrill

Chris Metzger

Hitendra Mishra

Tao Mi

Avi Moghaddam

Gus Monico

Richard Moreno

Robert Motoshige

Rashad Moumneh

Ali Mozayeni

Art Munda

Lisa Munro

Mark Murphy

Susan Murray

Omar Nasir

Sander
  Nauenberg

Dustin Neal

Mitch Needleman

Ali Nemat

Ben Newcott

Danny Nguyen

Yutaka Nishida

Andrew Niu

Alex Norman

Jay Novak

Shawn O'Connell

Sam Osborn

Scott Padelsky

Archana
  Panukonda

Brady Park

Daniel Penrod

Doug Petrikat

Mike Pitta

Michael Poirier

Brennan Price

Haralampos
  Psichogios

Chris Purvis

Rajiv Rajpurkar

Scott Riccardella

Jason Richardson

Cecile Richardson

Praveen Rikkala

Jeff Root

Michael Saeedi

Toru Sakata

Irina Saulea

Amit Saxena

Dominic Schaffer

Susie Schmitt

Dmitry Schmoys

Mark Searight

Kim Sentovich

Max Seraj

Mihir Shah

Hemant Sharma

Kane Shieh

Marc Shioya

Brett Shipman

Kyle Shoren

Abhijeet
  Shrikhande

Napatorn Schulz

Todd Sigler

Alex Simampo

Scott Simpson

Abhi Singh

Vitas Sipelis

Rebecca Smith

Kevin Smylie

Matrin Sobczak

Vihang Solanki

Ryan Solomon

Sachin Sontakke

Alex Stania

John Stedfield

Kojiro Sugiura

Kamran Syed

Katrin Szardenings

Matt Tappan

Matt Tarka

Kevin Tays

Kevin Teets

Ariel Tonnu

Dietmar Trees

Mitch Tsai

Dennis Ulrich

Ben Uy

Mike Vachani

Kyri Van Hoose

Luis Vasquez

Krishna
  Venugopal

Apoorva Verma

Kate Vezzetti

Beth Walls

James Walsh

Jessica Wang

Rick Warner

Ilan Weinberg

Katherine Wells

Tim Wilton

Jennifer Wold

Phillis Wong

Erin Worland

Silvia Wu

Joyce Wu

Weiya Xiao

Charles Xie

Calor Yan

Jeff Yang

Po Yang

Hani Yassin

Sohmin Yee

Clinton Yip

Steve Yoon

Chris Yount

Paul Yuhas

David Zeng

Er Zhang

Catherine Zhou

Merage Students Who Worked on Cases Related to the Crash of 2007 to 2009

Steve Alexson
Awab Ali
Jim Annes
Pam Arends-King
Spencer Arnold
Amir Bagherpour
Prabhu
  Balashanmugam
Lisa Baldewin
Tara Ballman
Miguel Bernal
Andy Bi
Vern Briggs
Matt Brinker
Juan Campo
Glen Chang
William Chang
Ben Chen
Brandon Chen
Vincent Cheng
Jeff Clark

Karin Conroy
Anderson Crosby
Jayson Crouch
Neelam Dave
Jon Dvorak
Gnanam Elumalai
Erick Flores
Evan Gates
Rick Goddard
Guillermo Gower
Peter Grant
Vicki Grubbs
Raj Gupta
Jeff Hanks
Tarif Hawasly
Rainy Hsia
Michael Huang
Chris Hughes
Hemant Jindal
Golam Kabir
Ken Kenjale

John Kim
Howard Ko
Girish Kripalani
Jeff Kvech
Jay Lahita
Ryan Lan
Mari Larios
Mengchen Li
Brian Liang
Joe Lin
Joy Lin
Ruel Macaraeg
Nora Makhsudova
Jay Mandavia
Jasdeep Mann
Kim McGrath
Brian Nadel
Fredy Orellana
Amy Osajima
Min Pae
Gloria Park

Michael Perlongo
Jean Platt
Gene Powell
Shankara
  Raghuraman
Matt Rhead
Reza Sabahi
Leila Samoodi
Noel Santillan
Sameer Shah
Roy Sharma
Laura Sheen
Devang Soparkar
Jane Terry
Daevin Thomas
Mark Tran
Chau Trieu
Ernie Trinidad
Randy Ulrey

Index